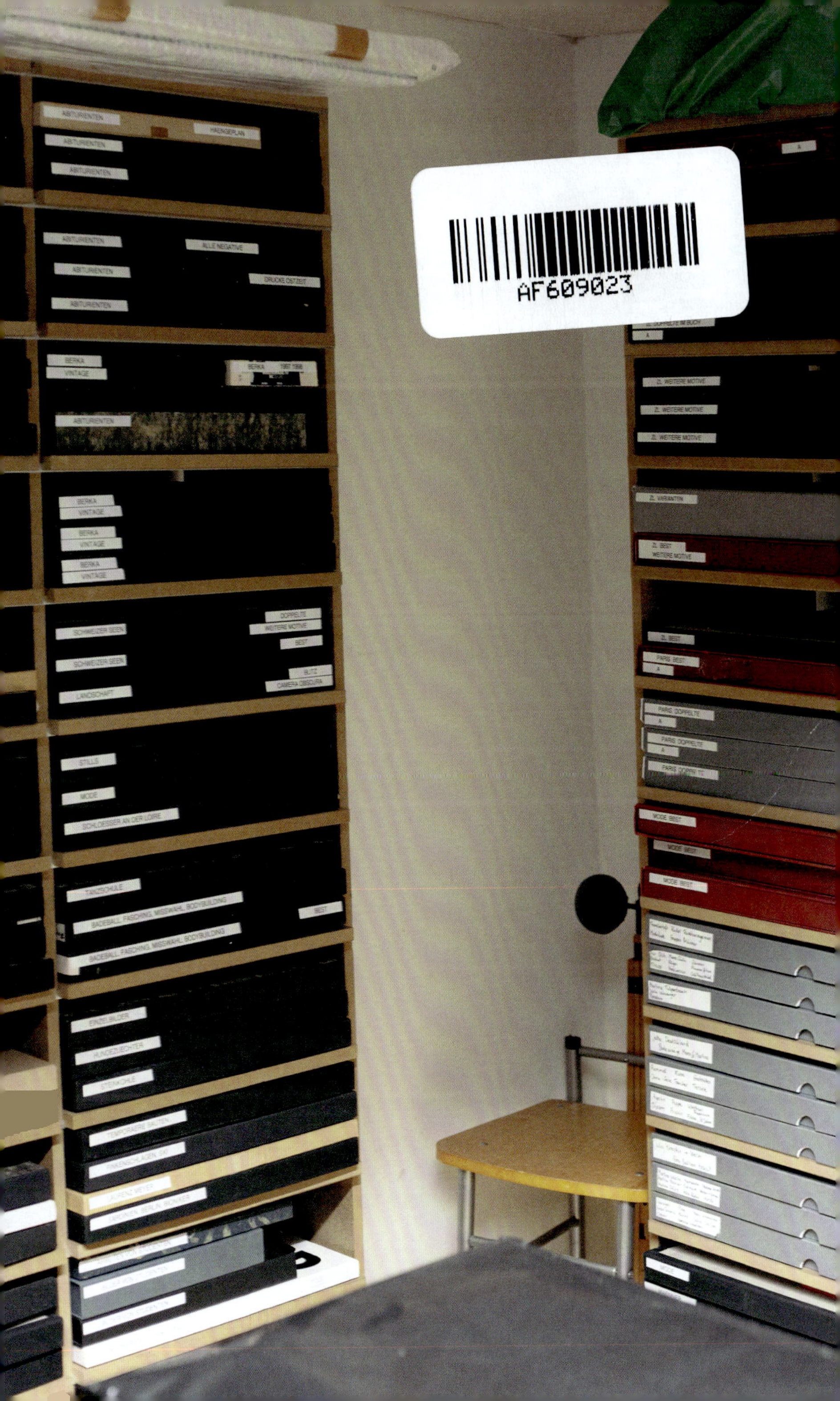
ABITURIENTEN
HAENGEPLAN
ABITURIENTEN
ABITURIENTEN
ABITURIENTEN
ALLE NEGATIVE
ABITURIENTEN
DRUCKE OSTZEIT
ABITURIENTEN
BERKA
VINTAGE
ABITURIENTEN
BERKA
VINTAGE
BERKA
VINTAGE
BERKA
VINTAGE
DOPPELTE
WEITERE MOTIVE
SCHWEIZER SEEN
BEST
SCHWEIZER SEEN
BLITZ
CAMERA OBSCURA
LANDSCHAFT
STILLS
MODE
SCHLOESSER AN DER LOIRE
TANZSCHULE
BADEBALL, FASCHING, MISSWAHL, BODYBUILDING
BEST
BADEBALL, FASCHING, MISSWAHL, BODYBUILDING
EINZELBILDER
HUNDEZUECHTER
STEINKOHLE
TEMPORAERE BAUTEN
ZL. WEITERE MOTIVE
ZL. WEITERE MOTIVE
ZL. WEITERE MOTIVE
ZL. VARIANTEN
ZL. BEST
WEITERE MOTIVE
ZL. BEST
PARIS BEST
PARIS DOPPELTE
PARIS DOPPELTE
MODE BEST
MODE BEST
MODE BEST

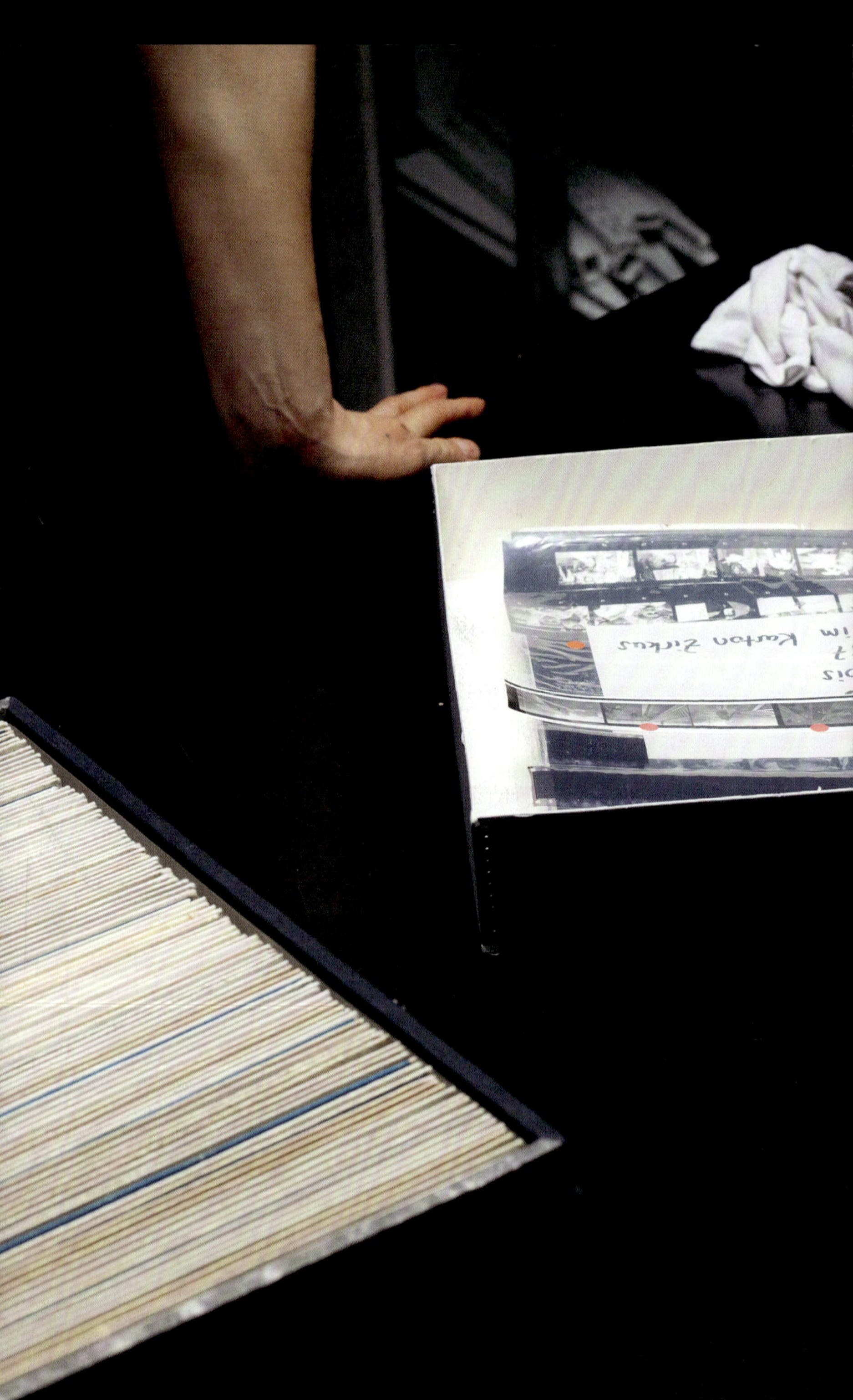
bis
7
im Karton Zirkus

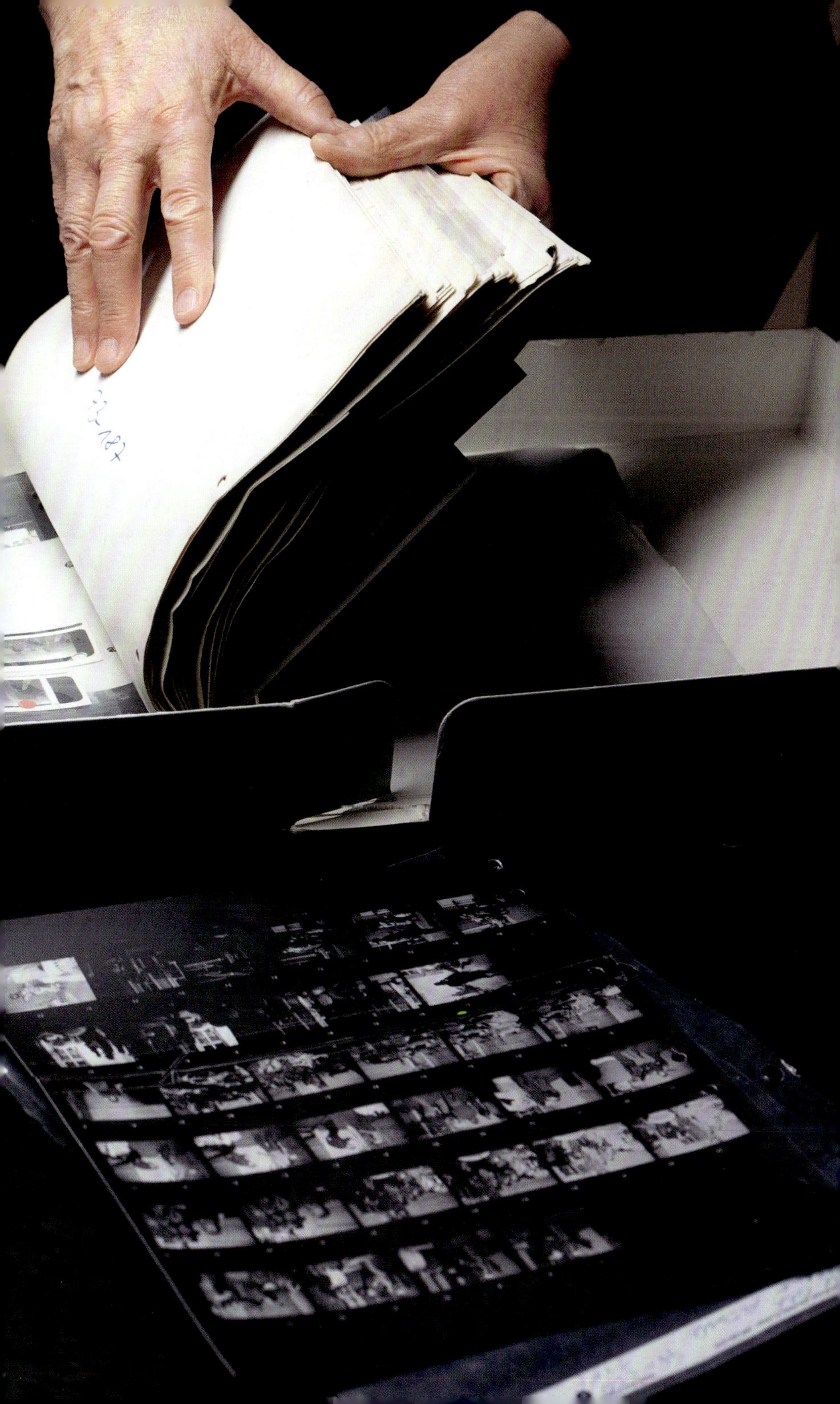

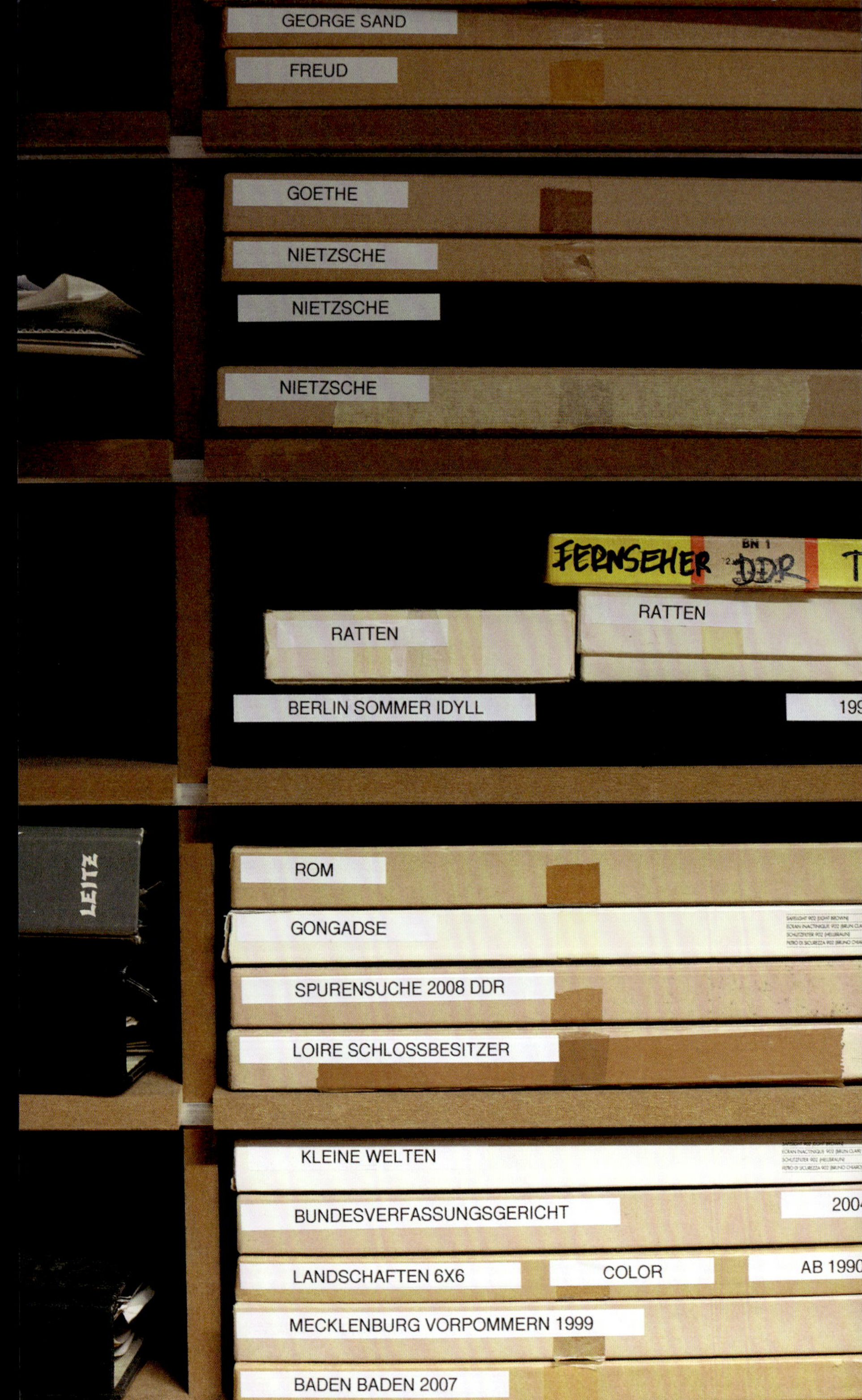
GEORGE SAND
FREUD
GOETHE
NIETZSCHE
NIETZSCHE
NIETZSCHE
FERNSEHER
BN 1
DDR
RATTEN
RATTEN
BERLIN SOMMER IDYLL
LEITZ
ROM
GONGADSE
SPURENSUCHE 2008 DDR
LOIRE SCHLOSSBESITZER
KLEINE WELTEN
BUNDESVERFASSUNGSGERICHT
LANDSCHAFTEN 6X6
COLOR
AB 1990
MECKLENBURG VORPOMMERN 1999
BADEN BADEN 2007

Ute and Werner Mahler, Lehnitz 2021

‘My ideal outcome is to find and shed light on something others have overlooked.’
PETER PILLER

‘We research and exhibit whatever’s accessible.’
BEATE GÜTSCHOW

‘I don’t operate with the term “oeuvre”. That’s for others to decide.’
ULRICH WÜST

‘You can’t shut the door on people seeing things differently in a hundred years’ time.’
FRIEDA AND LILY VON WILD, ESTATE SIBYLLE BERGEMANN

‘In general, I think it’s good to keep things fluid or open-ended.’
ANDREAS LANGFELD

‘What goes unseen is also part of a nation’s history.’
AKINBODE AKINBIYI

'It would be even less my style to issue precise guidelines for how to handle it.'
JOCHEN LEMPERT

'I understand the archive as a body, and I want to relate it to my body and set it in motion by artistic means.'
ÖZLEM ALTIN

'I think archives that are not digitised and made accessible online will increasingly fall into obscurity.'
ULRIKE KUSCHEL

'Especially now, in our digital age, it is essential to learn which images are important and which are not.'
ANNETTE KELM

'Having things that are worth seeing is a precious feeling.'
ELFIE SEMOTAN

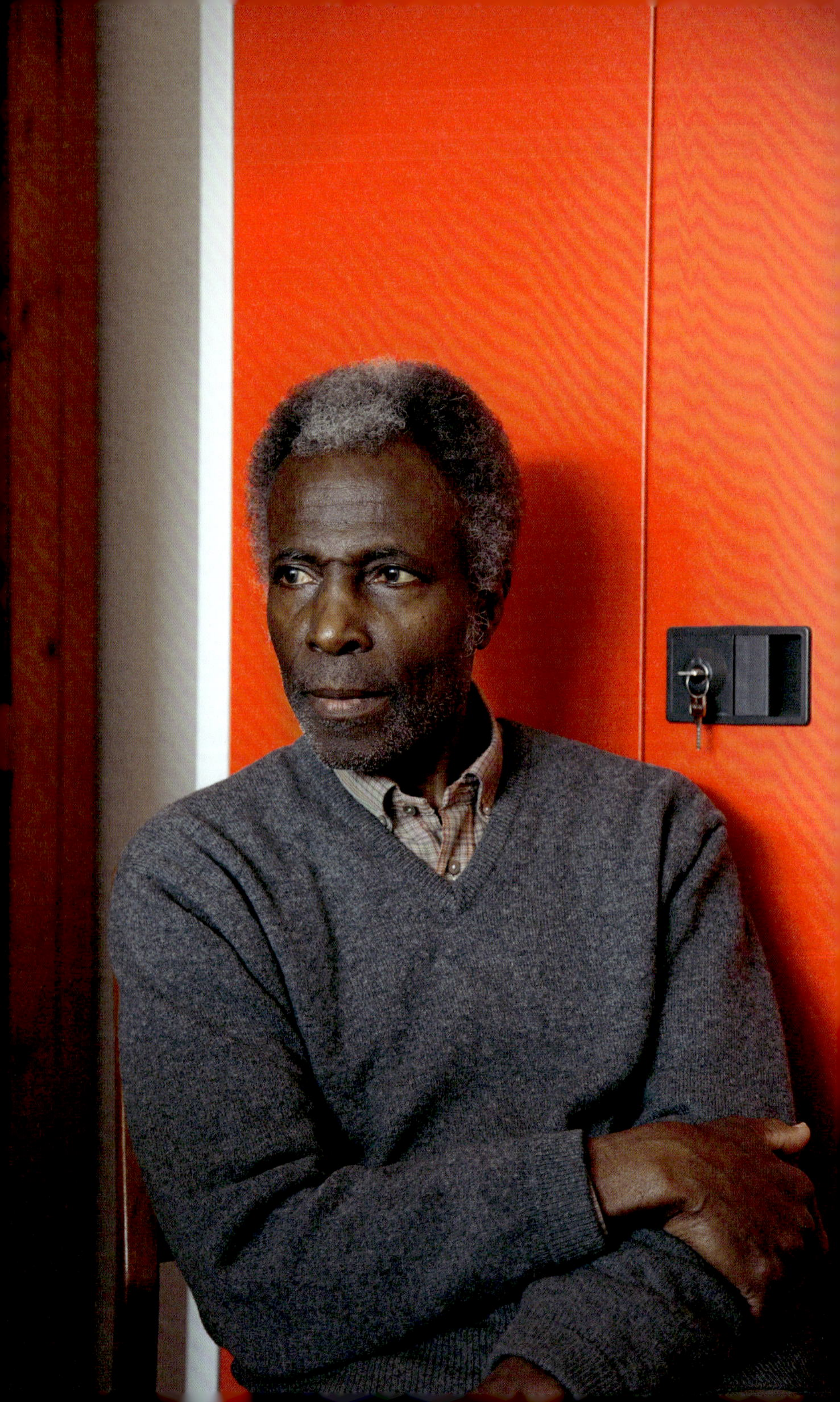

Akinbode Akinbiyi, Berlin 2021

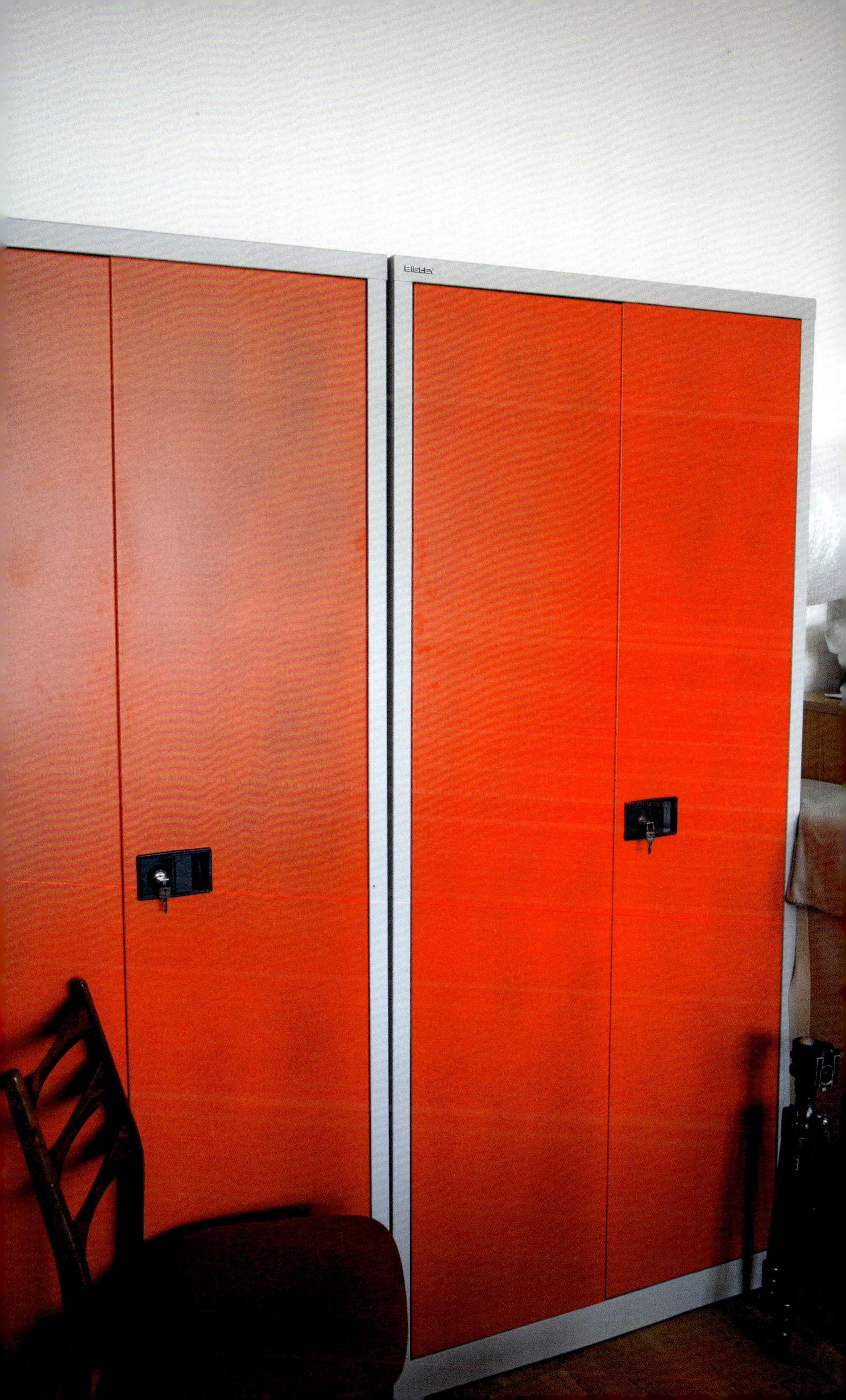
BISLEY

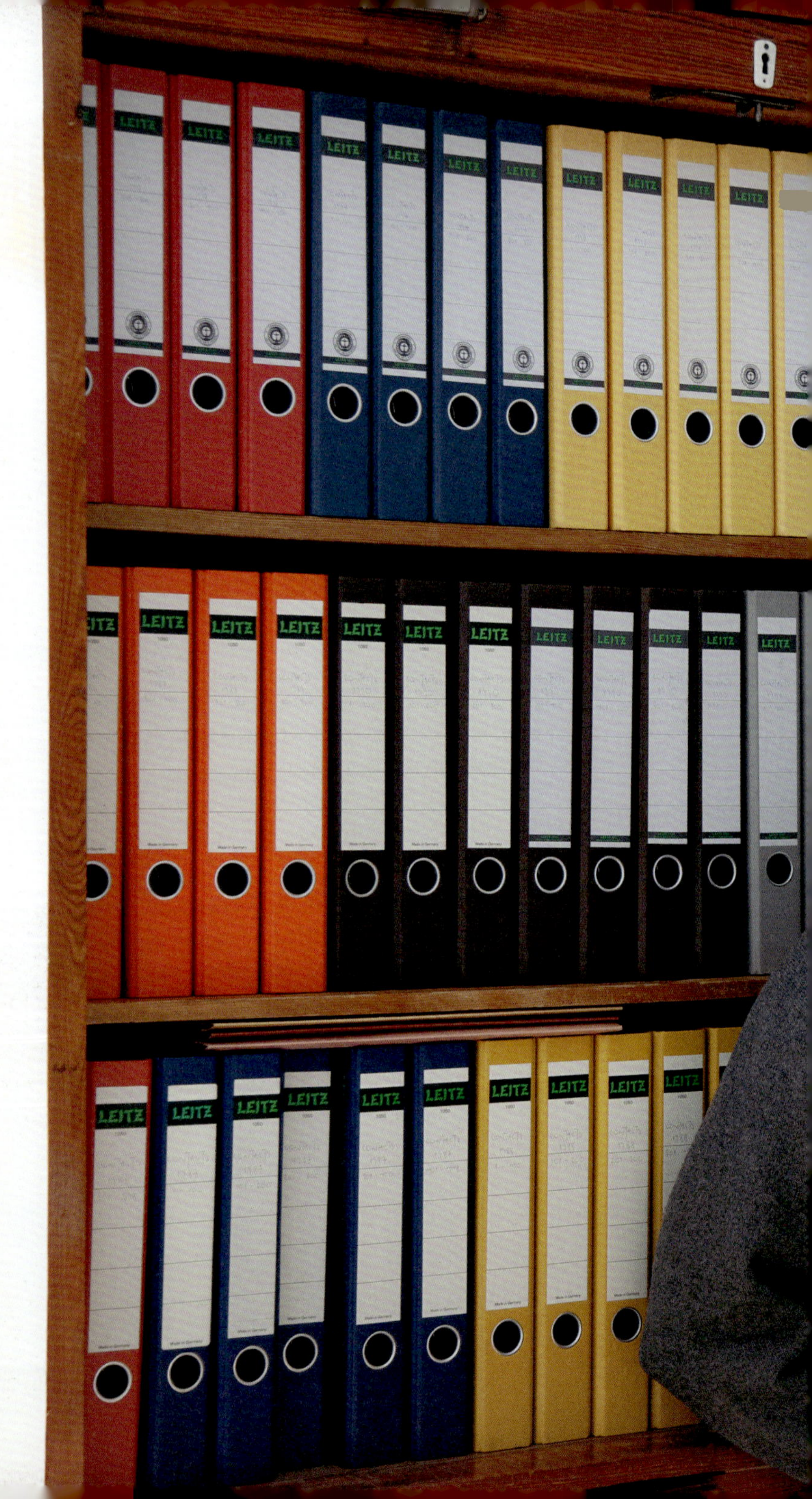
LEITZ

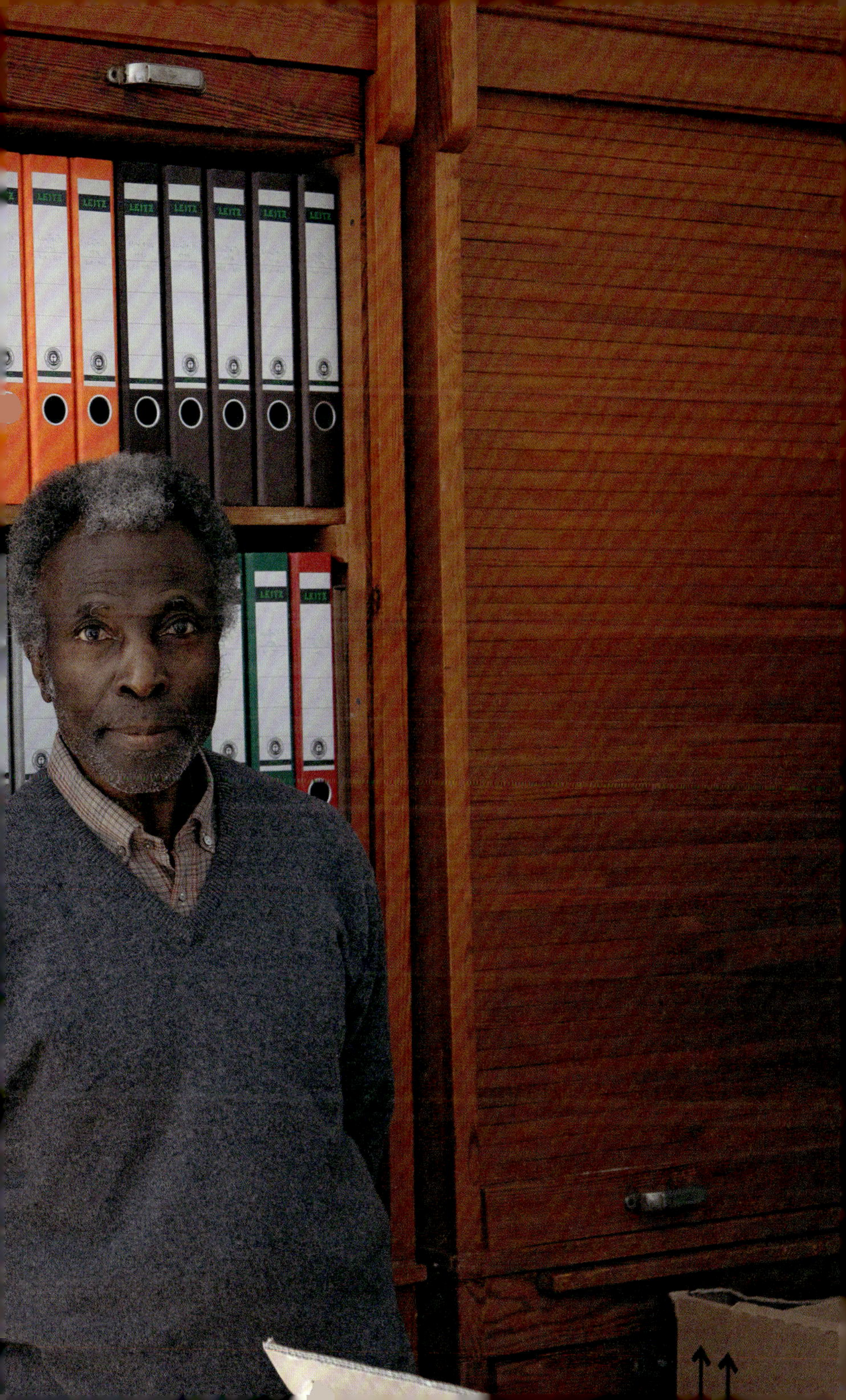

DISTANZ

Objects in Time

Lighting the Archive with Mike Sperlinger

KONTEXT

Contents

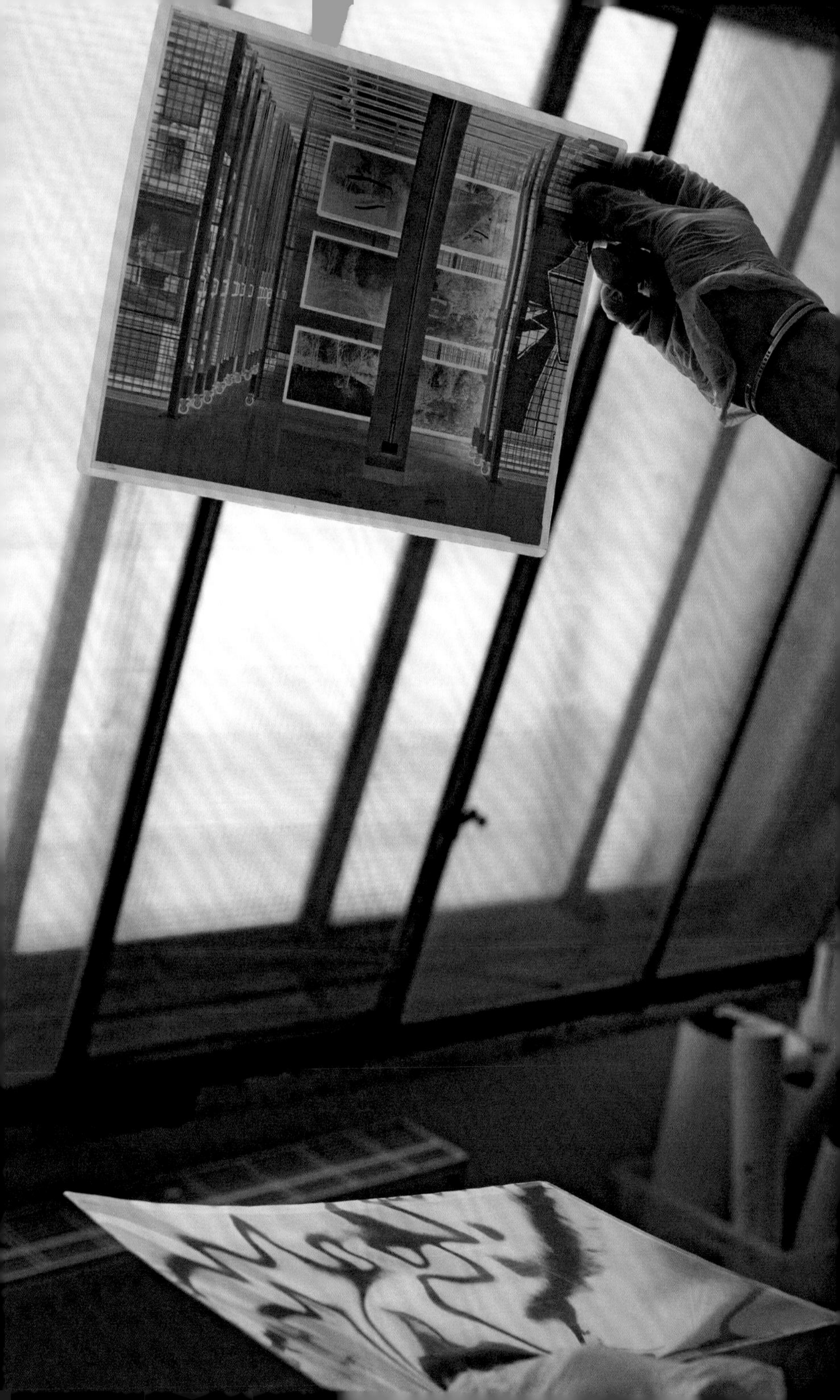

Sophie Thun, Vienna 2022

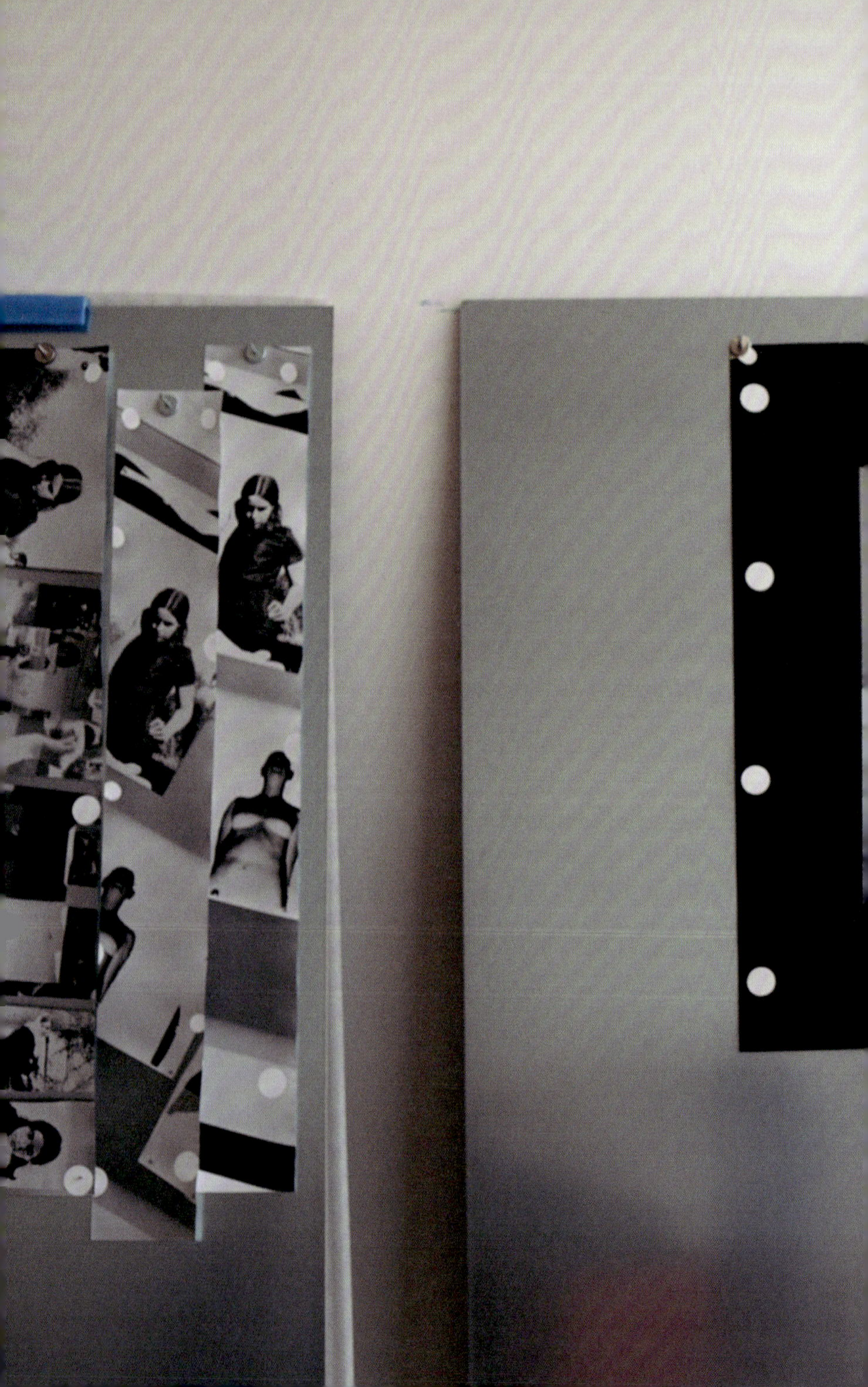

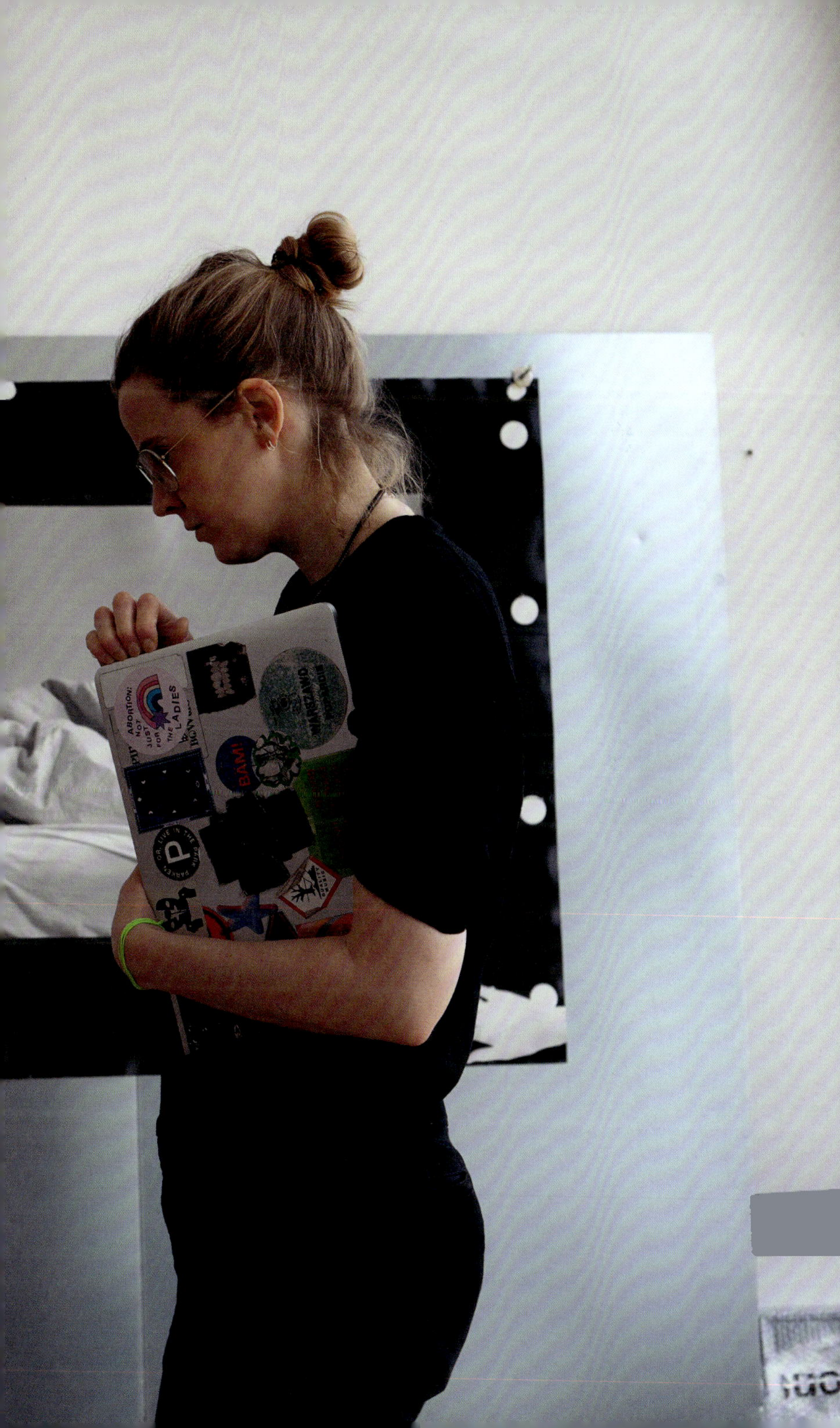
ABORTION: NOT JUST FOR THE LADIES
BAM!

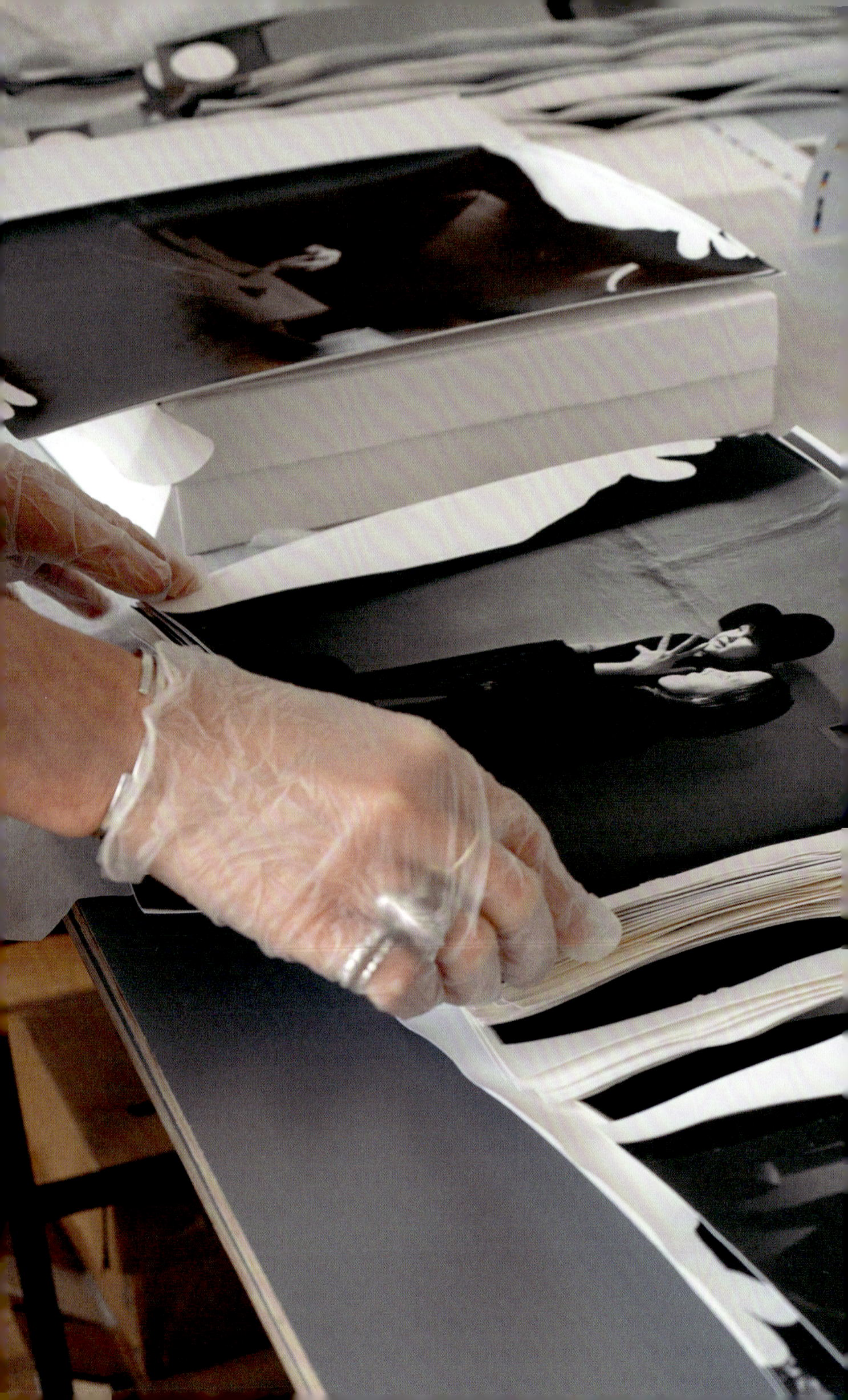

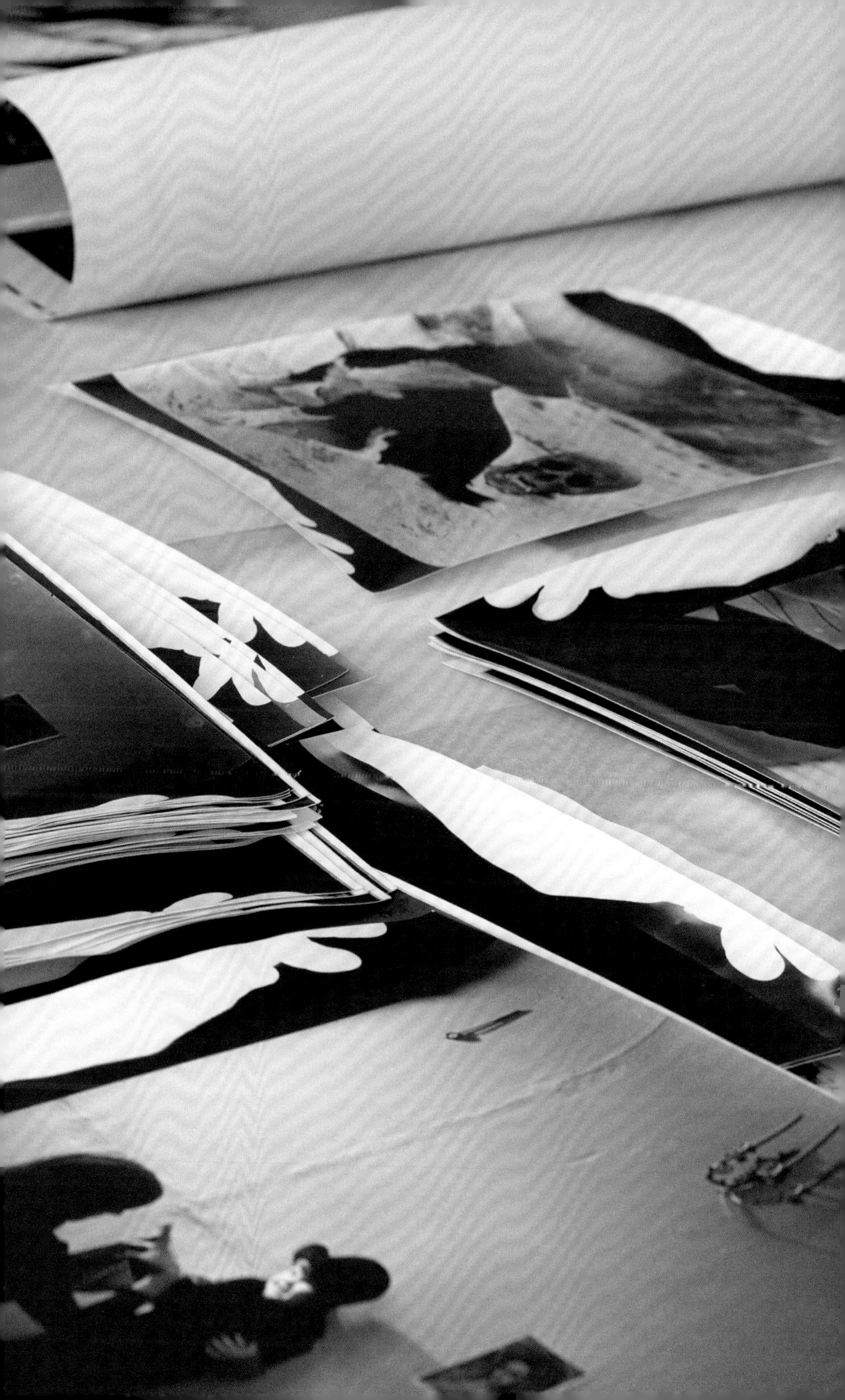

Note from the Editors

Matthias Kliefoth and Rebecca Wilton

In the fast-paced global art world, it is mainly the big names that receive attention, including extending beyond their own lifetime. But at the same time it also often happens that artworks are discovered and presented whose originators had temporarily fallen into oblivion. This may occur while the artist in question is still alive, or unknown and surprising works may emerge posthumously. Although the seismographic search for fresh talent and the promotion of promising, as-yet-unexploited careers are crucial to maintaining the art market system, such rediscoveries often possess a particularly inspiring complexity. Such a situation of researching and presenting forgotten works raises many questions on issues such as practical approaches, the need for legal clarification, and potential ethical or content-related conflicts.

In his essay 'Two Slight Returns', writer and curator Mike Sperlinger discusses the photographic oeuvre of German artist Marianne Wex and the series of pictures made by American photographer Chauncey Hare. Both bodies of work are based on a critical, sociological approach. In Wex's feminist practice, patriarchal power structures are exposed via an analysis of body image and posture, while Hare's pictures document the working class and its living and working spaces in the late 1960s and 1970s in the United States. Sperlinger takes both artists' decision to end their artistic career as a point of departure for exploring their lives in the art world. Having ended his photographic practice, the autodidact Hare decided to work in therapy. In the years after her art career, Wex sought out alternative forms of medicine for physical healing. In his essay, Sperlinger engages critically with the ways 'forgotten artists' are treated at a remove in time from their artistic activity, raising key questions about whether and how biographical influences and decisions can be included in this belated reception – or whether, on the contrary, they are uncomfortable or even questionable factors in processes of rediscovery and revaluation.

Lighting the Archive was founded in the context of discussions around a planned German Federal Institute for Photography to secure and preserve photographic estates. Although photographic art has increasingly entered museum collections since the 1990s, the safeguarding, conservation, and in-depth study of this key contemporary visual medium remains a challenge – not least due to insufficient institutional facilities and research options. Lighting the Archive conducts interviews that bring into the debate the voices of those whose work is crucial to an Institute for Photography: the photographers themselves. The following questions provide an initial framework for conversations which then take on shapes of their own: How do photographers deal with their material? What kind of archiving results from the respective visual practice? Is there an ordering system? How have visual and archiving practices changed since the digital turn? What form does an archive need in order to function as a system, and one that is also comprehensible to third parties if necessary? How does it need to be organised in order to convey knowledge? And what knowledge would that be? Is it possible to see the archive – once transferred to an institution – not only as storage but also as an instrument of research and education? And furthermore, how might one operate from within it?

Lighting the Archive spoke to Mike Sperlinger about how to deal with estates and bequests by living artists, about how important knowledge and assessment of biographic details are in the posthumous communication and presentation of artworks, and also about the place available for 'dissonant' or 'deviant' artistic practices in a field dominated by canon-building constellations of power. As well as specific approaches to the work of Wex and Hare, Sperlinger also discusses his experience as co-founder of LUX, a film archive in London, and as one of those looking after the estate of artist, writer, and curator Ian White (1971–2013) who poses a challenge to this process with his practice based on multiple media and especially performance. The photographs in this publication were taken during Lighting the Archive's interviews and give insights into the photographers' workspaces and organisational structures.

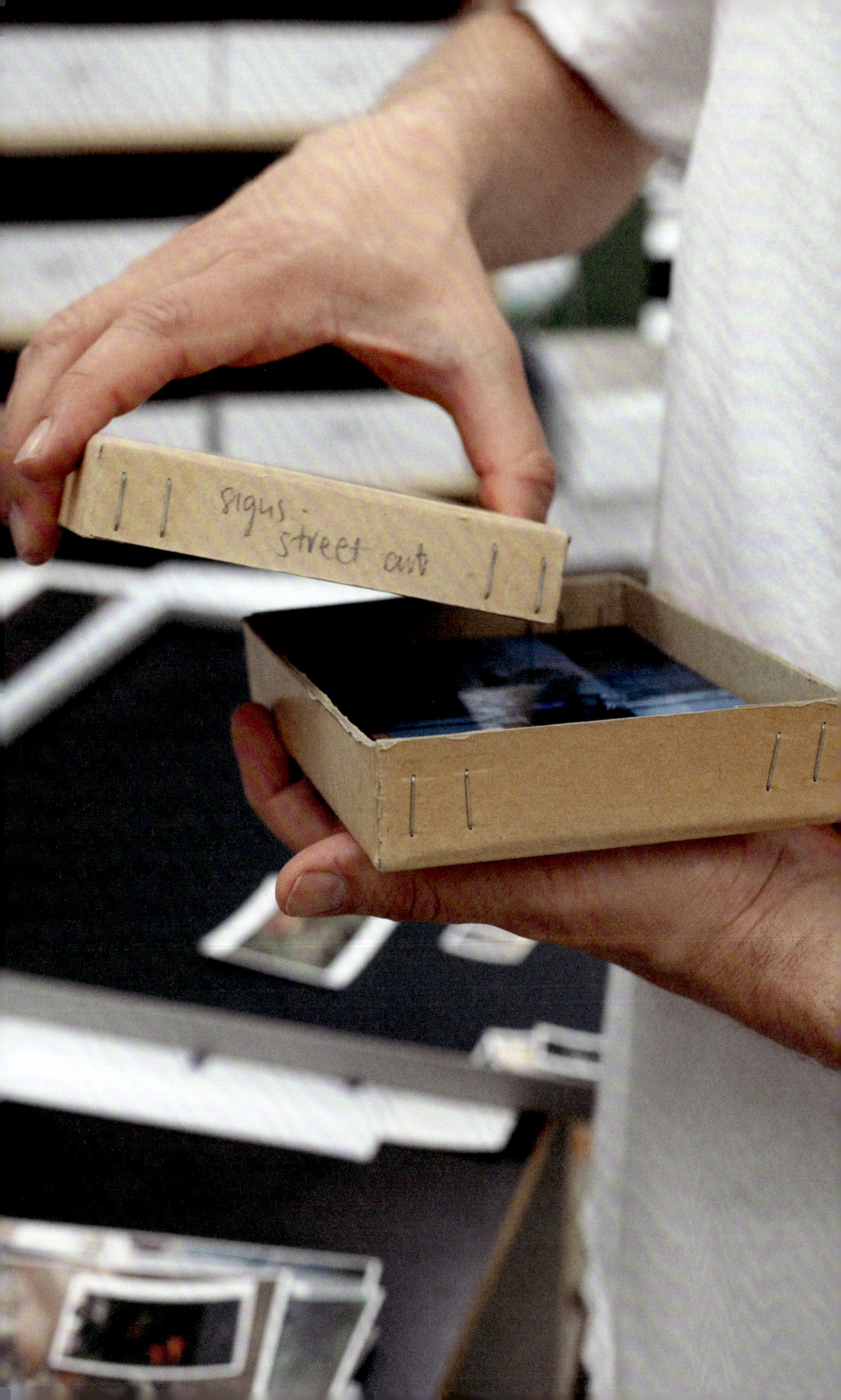
signs -
street art

Wolfgang Tillmans, Berlin 2021

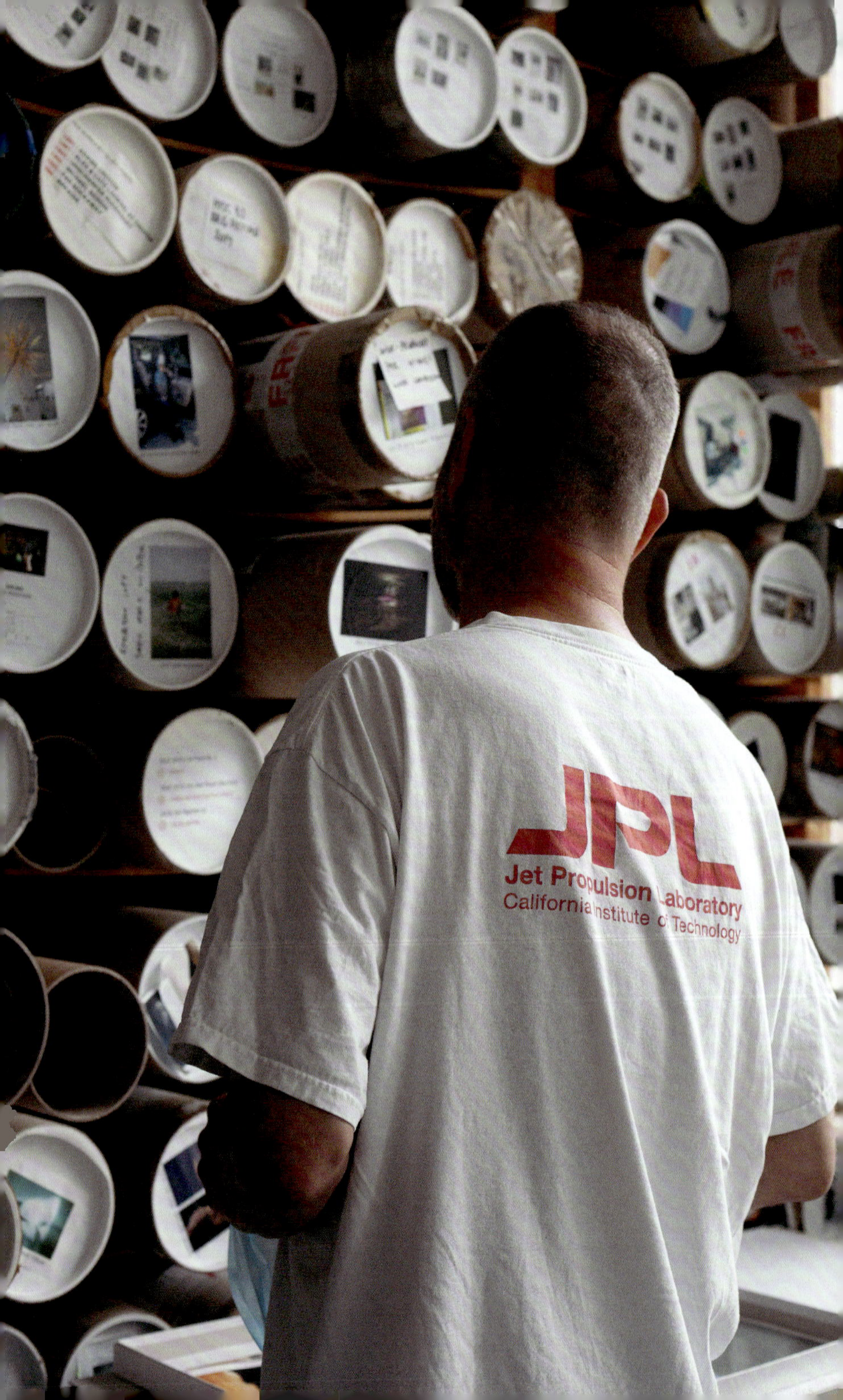
JPL
Jet Propulsion Laboratory
California Institute of Technology

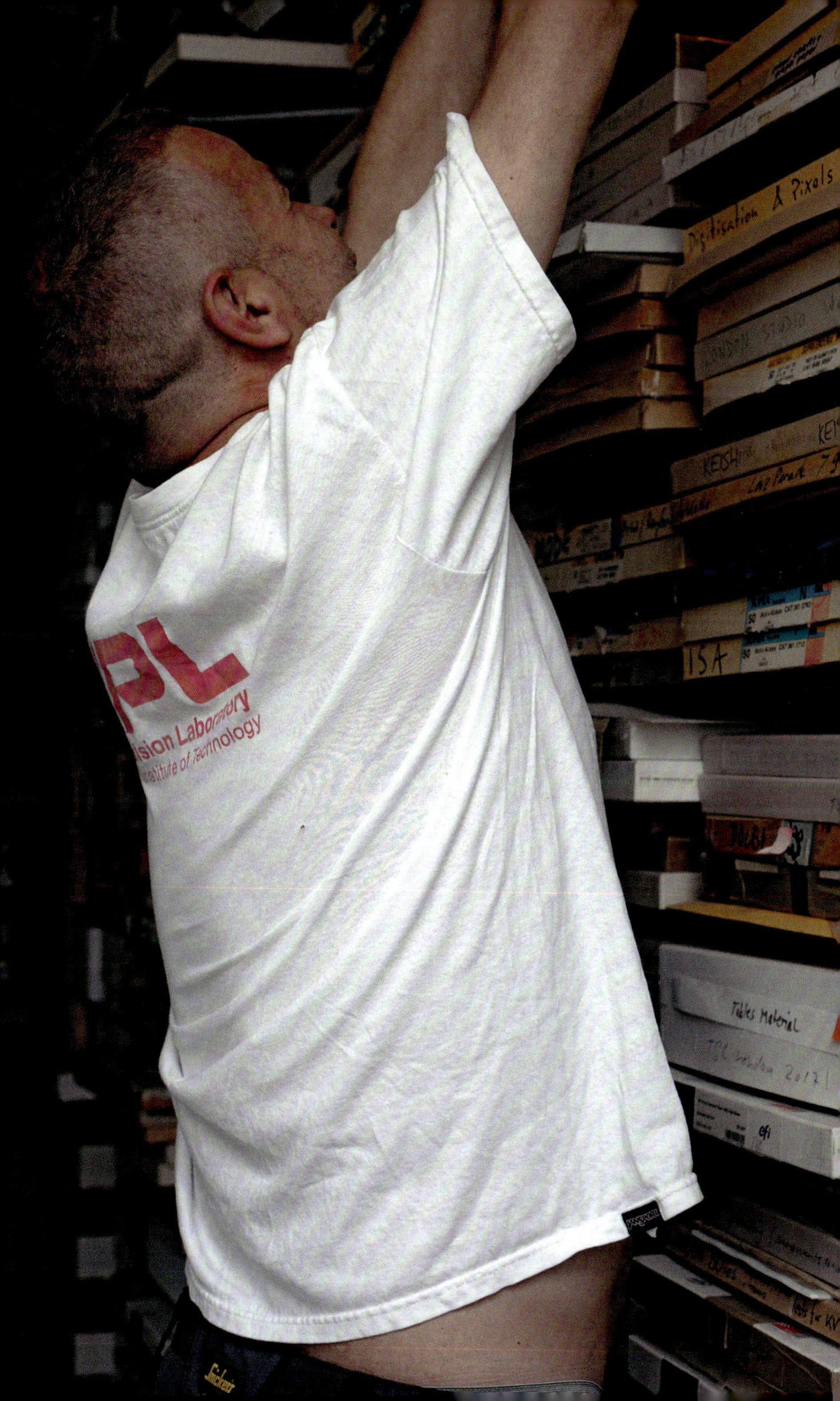
Digitisation & Pixels
Titles Material

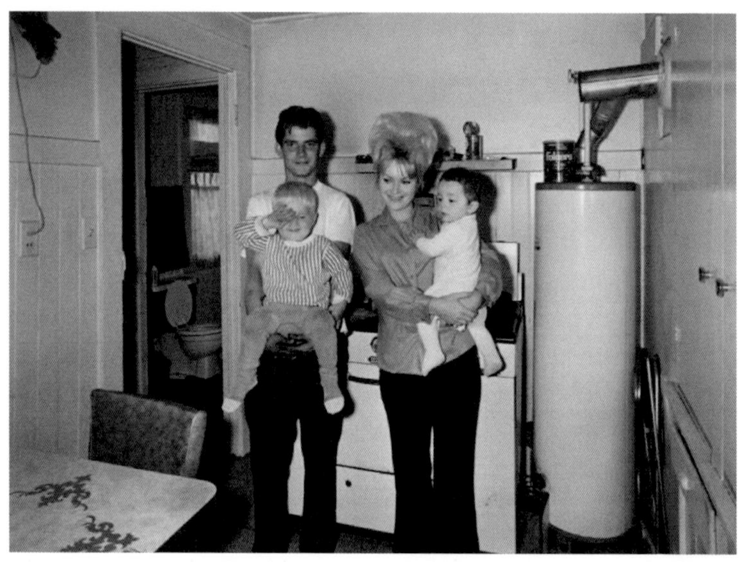

Chauncey Hare, *Richmond, California,* 1969

These photographs were made by Chauncey Hare to protest and warn against the growing domination of working people by multi-national corporations and their elite owners and managers.

Two Slight Returns: Chauncey Hare and Marianne Wex

Mike Sperlinger

Writing about the poet Aidan Andrew Dun, Iain Sinclair laid out a contradictory double-imperative: 'The poet has a dual responsibility: to give himself over entirely to his work, and to stage-manage a career.'[1] The formula is quintessentially Sinclairian: Romantic realpolitik. The first imperative might seem more palatable than the second, which it in any case excludes with that 'entirely' – but only if we prefer our poets, or artists, to have vocations rather than careers.

For Chauncey Hare and Marianne Wex, the question of a career, of art as a profession, was unresolved in ways which have affected the legacy of their work, and even the legitimacy of applying the category of 'artist' to them. While they were contemporaries, making their most important work in the 1970s, they had little else obviously in common: Hare was a documentary photographer based in California; Wex was an artist and art teacher living in Hamburg. They never met, or exhibited together, nor were they even aware of one another's work. But in their choices, the vicissitudes of their reputations, and the political valencies of their work, there are parallels which suggest how vocations can unhinge careers, and how giving oneself over entirely to the work might mean abandoning it altogether.

When Chauncey Hare staged a one-man protest outside the exhibition 'Mirrors and Windows' at the San Francisco Museum of Modern Art in 1979, he seemed to be entirely neglecting Sinclair's second imperative. The curator Jack von Euw, who oversaw the 2009 publication of a new Steidl edition of Hare's work called *Protest Photographs*, recollects being handed a leaflet by Hare as he stood in line for a lecture by the show's curator: 'I read his text and it crossed my mind that he was a lunatic.' Hare was protesting, amongst other things, against Philip Morris's sponsorship of the show and the inclusion of one of his own images in it.

To von Euw, encountering Hare for the first time, it appeared to be straightforward 'career suicide'.[2]

Hare started out as a landscape photographer in his spare time, while working at the Chevron oil company in California. His experiences during a work assignment in Mississippi during the civil rights upheavals of 1967 were transformative, for both his politics and his photography, and the following year he began a series of portraits of people in their homes which became an exhibition and later a book, both with the title *Interior America*. Working in Oakland, California and the Sierra foothills, and subsequently in the Ohio valley where he had grown up, Hare focussed mostly, though not exclusively, on working class homes; shooting with a wide-angle lens, his images divide their attention equally between the inhabitants and their decor. They are extraordinary photographs: compassionate but also formal and complex, constantly interested in the interiors as sets dressed for living, which are often themselves full of other framed images on the walls. Sometimes his subjects are posing, though rarely looking into camera; sometimes they asleep, or hypnotised by the glow of an out-of-shot television set.

Subsequently, Hare's focus shifted to the workplace and he took images at Chevron and around Silicon Valley, for a second book called *This Was Corporate America* (1985). But, despite receiving three Guggenheim grants to support his photography, he struggled to find teaching work and also found himself in conflict with his employers: he left Chevron, apparently after conflict over his documentation of the company's working practices, and was fired from a position at the Environmental Protection Agency, at least in part, Hare felt, because of a study he had conducted into employee morale. Having retrained as a family therapist, he became a specialist in workplace abuse and published a book on the subject with his partner Judy Wyatt. He abandoned photography entirely and his previous body of work remained in storage until 1999, when he entered protracted negotiations to donate it to a public institution. Hare's stipulations – that the work could never be sold and that it could only be exhibited alongside one of two explanatory statements[3] he had written – meant at least one museum turned his donation down, before van Jack von Euw secured it for the Bancroft Library at the University of California.

It is hard to think of many careers less stage-managed than Hare's. Even in the afterword to *Protest Photographs*, von Euw is frank about the element of self-sabotage: 'Chauncey was so intent on getting his message across that he seemed to be stifling any other interpretation or engagement with his work.'[4] Hare had always been acutely uncomfortable about the gap between the world of his subjects and the art world where their images circulated:

From the beginning, I knew that to receive photo grants I was expected to present my photographs in a formal art way without accompanying text and to allow each of my photos to be used as a work of art that stands alone [...] This formal art process dehumanized the photographs by turning them into purely aesthetic objects. It allowed and valued only that reality attributed and defined by the viewer.[5]

Hare identified himself with his subjects, and moreover identified his images with them too – selling prints, he said, 'would have felt like selling the people'.[6] Hare's images themselves, however, are more ambivalent than all this would suggest. Discussing how welcoming people generally were when he asked to photograph them in their homes, Hare writes: 'Easy entry meant I had a responsibility to honor what I saw and photographed – especially when I used a wide angle lens that took in more than what people thought I was photographing.'[7] Many of the images testify to that slight deception, and it is part of what makes them compelling, but it complicates, or qualifies, Hare's idea of responsibility. Similarly, Hare's close identification of the people with their images is strange insofar as they are not named in the captions (only the place and date of the photograph, when known). Their particularity slides into something else – Hare himself calls them 'archetypal images of America'.[8] *Protest Photographs* shimmers with the tension between the claim implied by its title and the much more classical, and irreducibly aesthetic, appeal of many of its images.

Around the same time that Hare was protesting outside SFMoMA, a very different photography book was published in Germany. It was by an artist called Marianne Wex and its full title was *'Let's*

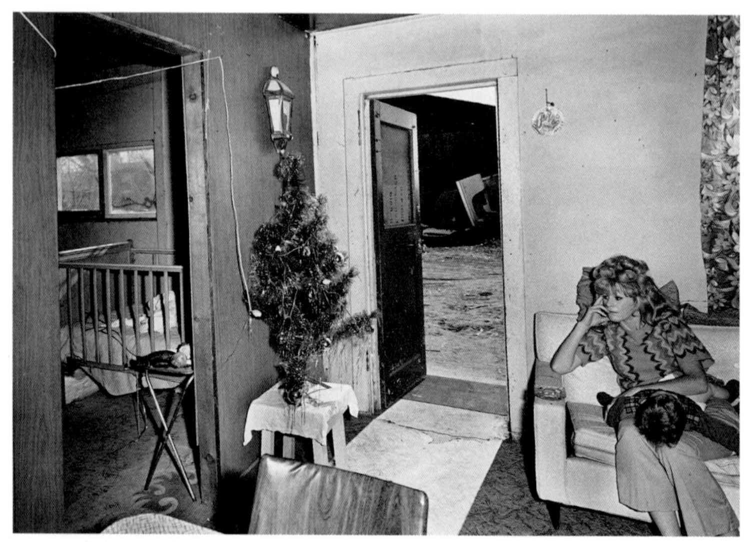

Chauncey Hare, *Richmond, California,* 1968–1970

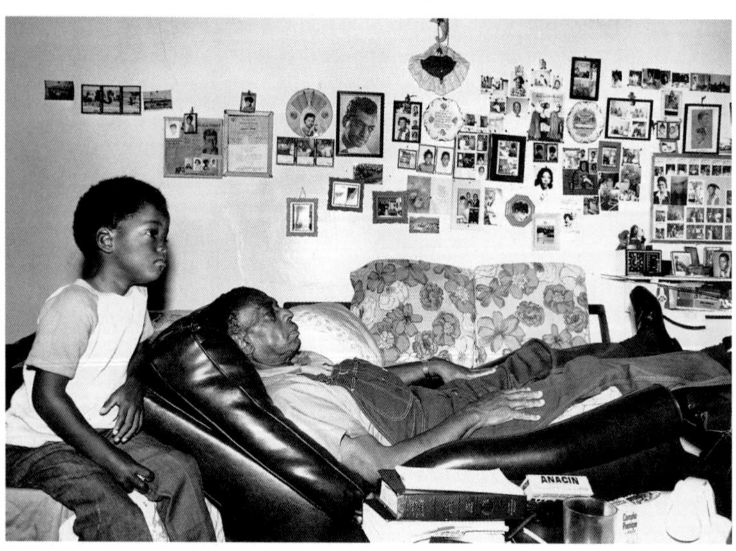

Chauncey Hare, *Richmond, California,* 1968–1970

Take Back Our Space': 'Female' and 'Male' Body Language as a Result of Patriarchal Structures (1979). Wex had started out as a painter, but an interest in body language had sent her out into the streets of Hamburg in the early 1970s with her Mamiya camera, where she had started to take pictures of people unawares at train stations and street crossings. After she had taken around 3,000 photographs, she began to sort them according to typologies of body language and to observe the differences between the sexes. While continuing to take more images, she also started to research ancient and mediaeval statuary as a record of previous era's 'ideals', and to plunder contemporary media images too.

Let's Take Back Our Space is organised thematically. The first half of the book focuses on contemporary images and groups them by posture ('Seated persons, leg and feet positions', 'Standing persons, arm and hand positions', etc.). On the left hand of each spread, images of men in a given posture run along the top and of women along the bottom; the right hand spread tends to be sparer, often reserved for one or two 'exceptions' to the stereotypically gendered gestures. The second half focuses on statuary and includes a number of short texts on art history, gender and socialisation, and accounts of Wex's own experiences.

As a whole, the book features a bewildering array of photographic source material: Wex's street photographs, photojournalism, advertisements, art historical reproductions, family album snapshots, pornography, mail order catalogue clippings, publicity shots, television and film stills, etc. Wex crops and juxtaposes the images purely according to their gestural content, and with a ruthless wit – for example, on page 102 we find a man standing on a field of bodies, Jewish victims of Nazi genocide, juxtaposed with, amongst others, a muscleman from a home exercise ad and a tourist on a Bangkok beach in similar poses. At such moments her work takes on an affinity with Hans-Peter Feldmann, otherwise a very different artist, while at other times there are clear parallels with feminist contemporaries like Martha Rosler and Sanja Iveković.

Like Hare, Wex's project derives part of its dynamic from its apparent contradictions. Its repetitions and reiterations can make the conventional postures it is resisting seem archetypal, inescapable; in defence of individuality, it presents serried ranks of stereotypes. There is something of Hare, too, in the vestigial echo

Leg and feet positions

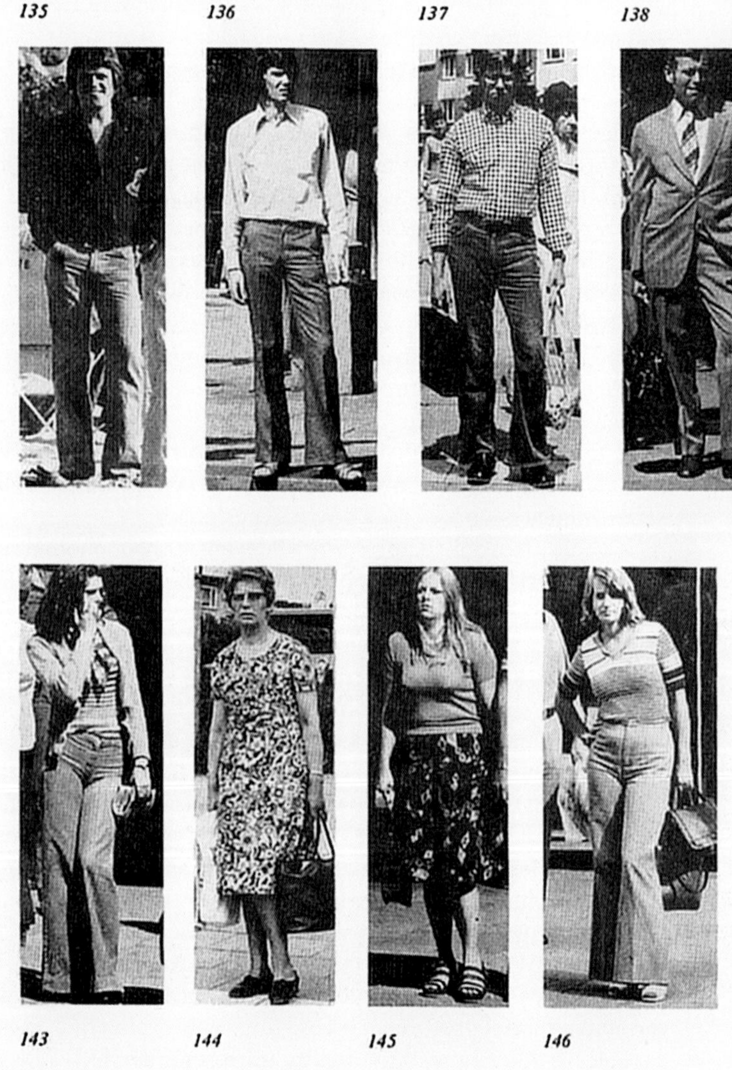

Marianne Wex, *'Let's Take Back our Space': "Female" and "Male" Body Language as a Result of Patriarchal Structures* (Frauenliteraturverlag Hermine Fees, 1979)

dvertisement for
ce copy machine
piegel 44/1975
39

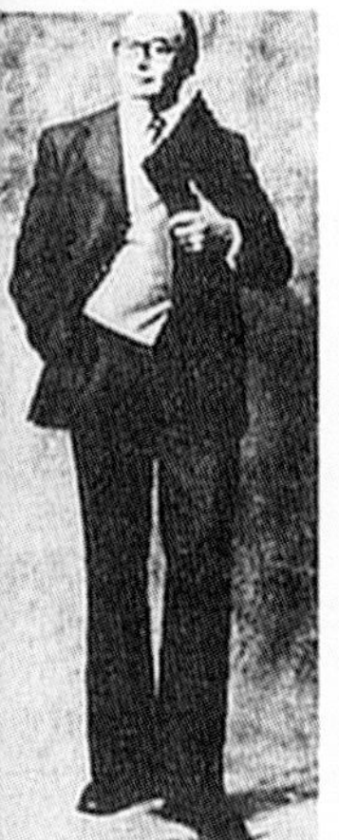

TV editor
E. Thomas
Stern 47/1975
140

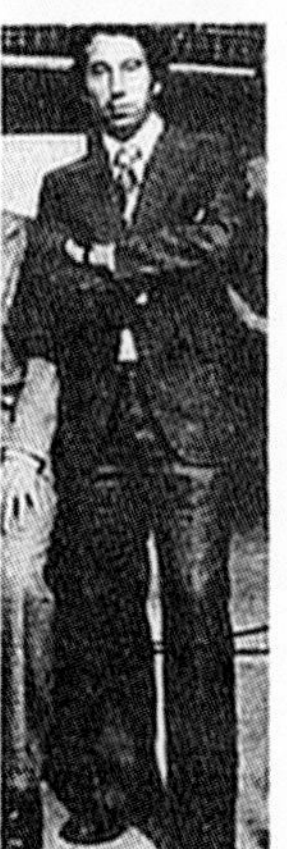

Advertisement for
"Big Jim",
Mattel GmbH,
Karstadt, Hamburg 1973
141

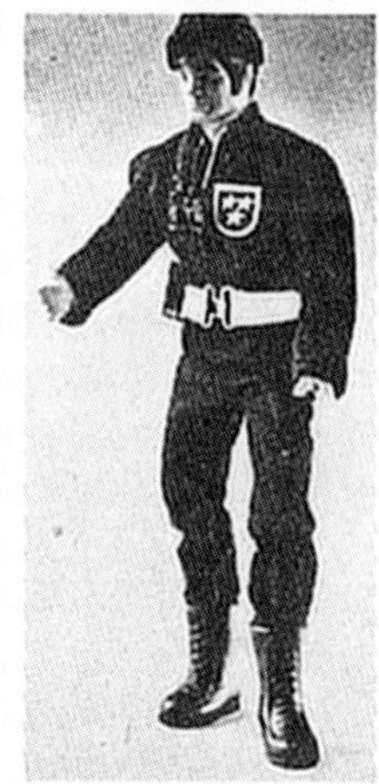

Actor Peter Falk
Photo: Universal-Television
and Columbia
Brigitte 4/1976
142

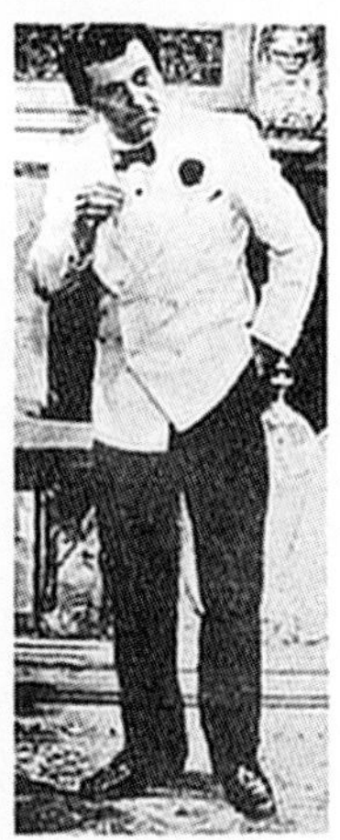

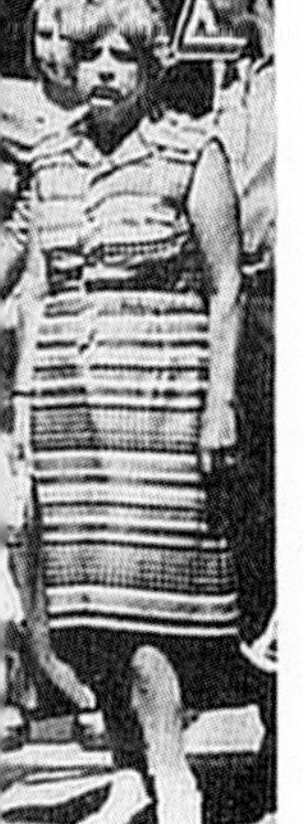

47

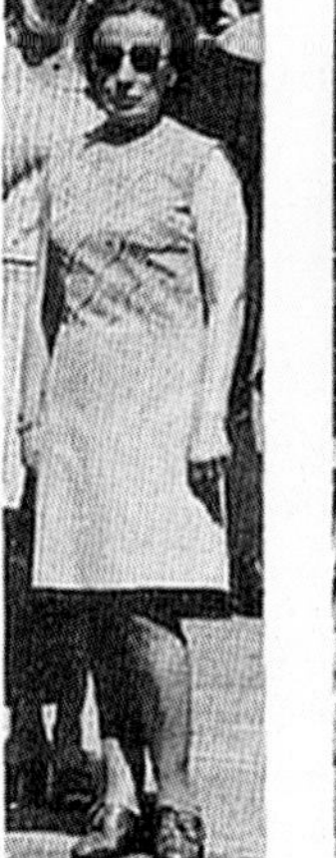

148

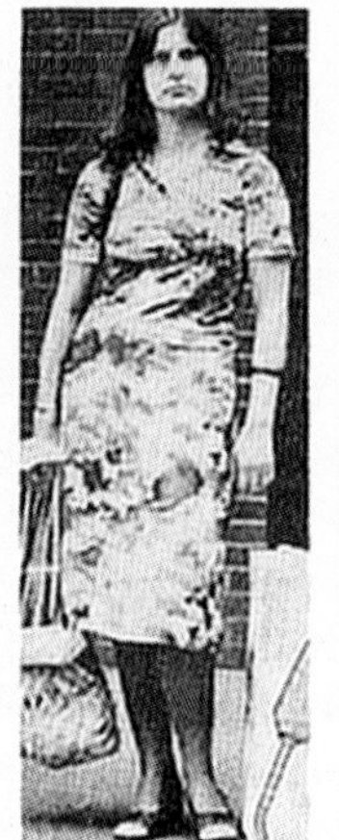

149

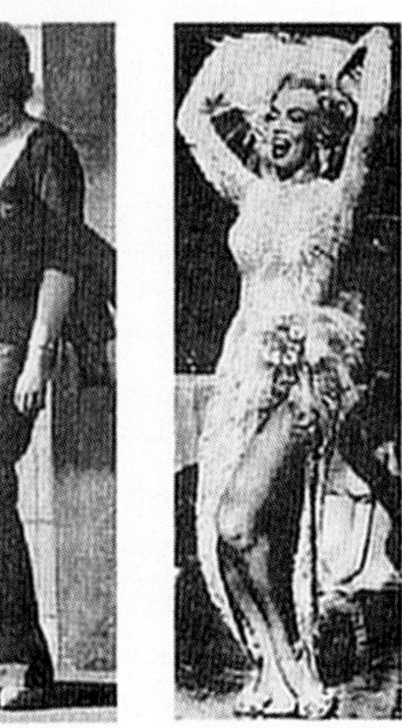

150

151
Marilyn Monroe

of voyeurism: if his images encompass more than his subjects were aware of, hers were, for the most part, completely unwitting (which was necessary, as she pointed out, to capture unconscious postures). And its sheer exhaustiveness is offset by its idiosyncratic categorisations, the exuberant subjectivity of its taxonomies. This last characteristic was something Wex was very conscious of, and understood as an attempt to overcome the separation between the sciences and everyday existence: 'knowledge is gathered in single fields without checking the relationships within the individual fields. And all of this happens while bracketing out the so-called personal feelings'.[9]
Wex's project originally took the form of dozens of large collaged panels, which were first exhibited as part of 'Künstlerinnen International 1877–1977' at NGBK in Berlin in 1977. It was well received and various elements of it were included in shows internationally over the following years, including one at the ICA in London in the early 1980s. Wex, however, was already turning away from her art practice by the time the book version of her work was published. Around the beginning of the period when she began making *Let's Take Back Our Space*, Wex had been diagnosed with a life-threatening illness; after the book was published she travelled widely and investigated alternative medicine, during which time her condition worsened before finally going into remission. Subsequently, she studied for several years under a natural healer called Lily Cornford in London, and for the last two decades she has given seminars on self-healing to small groups of women all around Europe, often drawing on what she felt she had learnt during the 1970s about the effects of comportment on women's physical and mental health. Her work served her as a teaching aid, while remaining otherwise out of circulation.

In many ways, Wex's project was diametrically opposed to Hare's. Hare was concerned, ostensibly at least, with individuals, whereas Wex was interested in patterns and stereotypes; Hare's images are expansive, trying to register every incidental detail, whereas Wex's are reduced and cropped to serve illustrative purposes (some are reversed horizontally, for example, to make the homologies clearer); Hare's subjects are always located within space, whereas the only locus for Wex's is their own bodies; and so on.

What the two share, nevertheless, is a kind of career trajectory: from increasingly politicised art-making to an abandonment of the role of artist altogether in favour of therapeutic practices, in the broadest sense. Hare, as well as setting himself in opposition to the 'formal art process', rejects even the label of 'photographer': 'I do not now see myself as a "photographer," but as a working person who has made photographs for a short period of his life.'[10] Wex, for her part, 'didn't mind if it was called art, any art to me is research'.[11] Feeling that almost all of the artistic and conceptual tools she had inherited were derived from patriarchal forms, she resolved to, 'put all my energies in creating new forms with other women [and] stop concerning myself with the analysis of the world of men'.[12]

Abandoning art, importantly, is not the same as apostasy. Neither Hare nor Wex has taken the well-established anti-career path of the wayward *poète maudit*, glorious renunciation; we are a long way from Rimbaud giving up poetry for gun-running. Hare and Wex both seem to have felt vocations ('the signals that came from inside', as Hare puts it) that called them through and then beyond art, at a moment when 'socially-engaged' or 'research-based' practices were not on the career menu for artists – while at the same time more contingent factors (conflict at work, illness) affected their choices. Their subsequent abandonment of art practice, and of any stage-managing of their erstwhile art careers, in each case helped to condemn their considerable bodies of work to relative obscurity. In fact, their subsequent careers perhaps retroactively contributed to this process too: therapy and healing are things contemporary art tends to keep at arm's length, perceiving them as too connected to ideas of instrumentalised self-expression and catharsis.[13]

Reviewing *Interior America* for the New Yorker in 1979, Janet Malcolm compared it to Walker Evans and Robert Frank's work, but concluded cautiously, 'it is too early to tell about Hare's place in photography'.[14] For over two decades that place has been very marginal. It is only fairly recently, with the Steidl publication and the first exhibition of Hare's work in Europe – some of the *Interior America* images featured in the show 'Anonymes', curated by David Campany and Diane Dufour, at Le Bal in Paris (2010) – that Hare's work has begun to receive

Pre-Roman and Roman sculptures. Seated figures

7th century BOT
pre-Roman,
Etruscan,
Rome, Palazzo
dei Conservatori
1

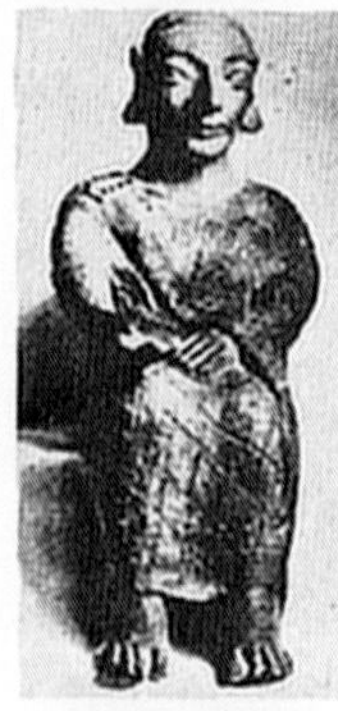

This sculpture is labeled "male" in a number of books, in others it is not sexually defined. It appears quite questionable to me that this is really a man.

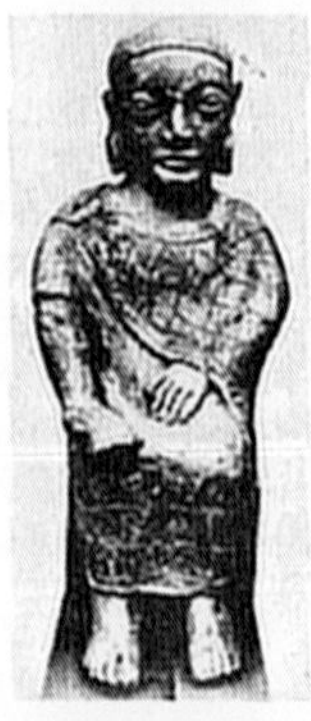

11
7th century BOT
Figure of a woman
pre-Roman,
Etruscan,
London,
British Museum

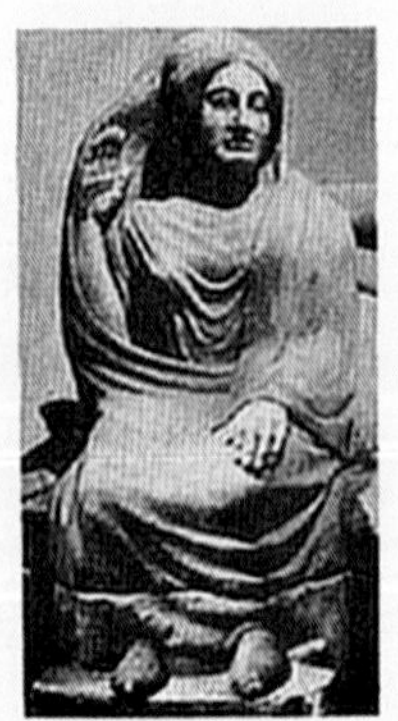

12
4th century BOT
Figure of a woman,
pre-Roman,
Etruscan,
Florence
Museo Archeologico

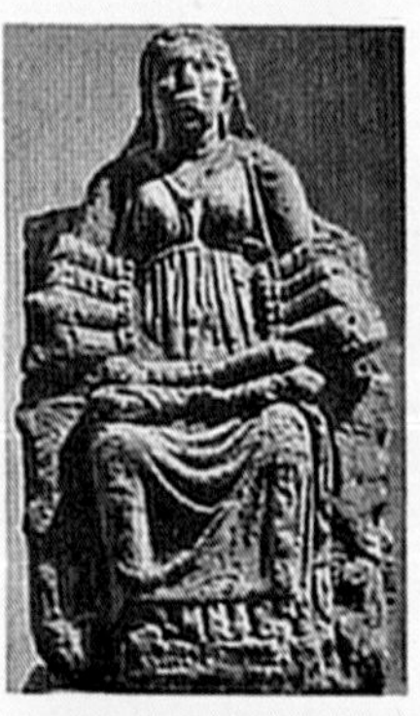

13
3rd century BOT
Votive statue of a woman
pre-Roman,
Capua, Museo Campano

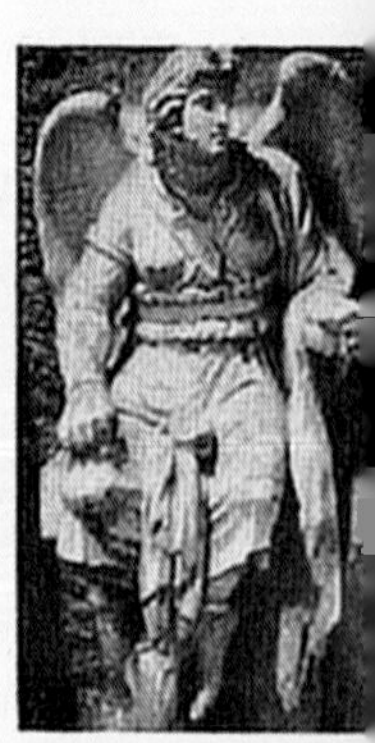

14
About 150 -125 BOT
Figure of a woman,
pre-Roman,
Etruscan,
Volumnii grave

Marianne Wex, *'Let's Take Back our Space': "Female" and "Male" Body Language as a Result of Patriarchal Structures* (Frauenliteraturverlag Hermine Fees, 1979)

2nd century BOT
Orpheus
pre-Roman,
Etruscan,
Palazzo dei
Conservatori
2

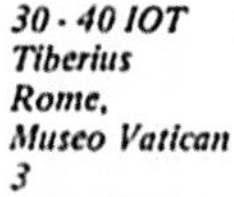

30 - 40 IOT
Tiberius
Rome,
Museo Vatican
3

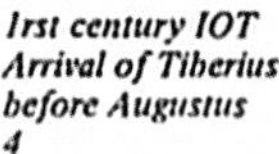

Irst century IOT
Arrival of Tiberius
before Augustus
4

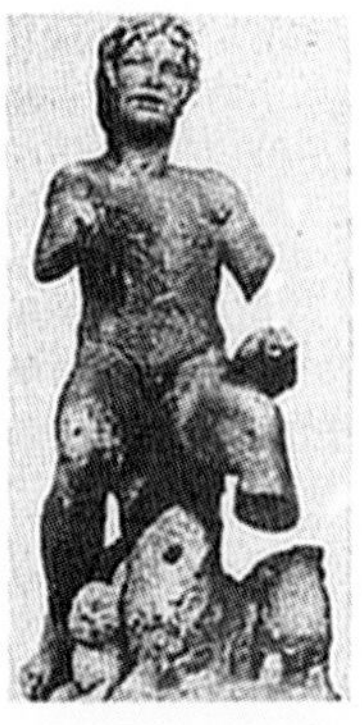

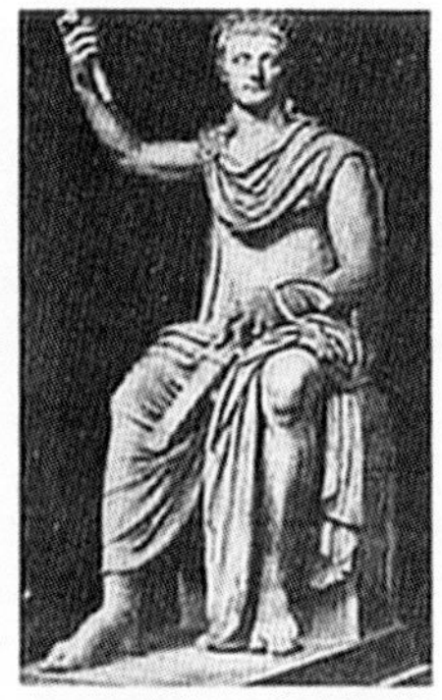

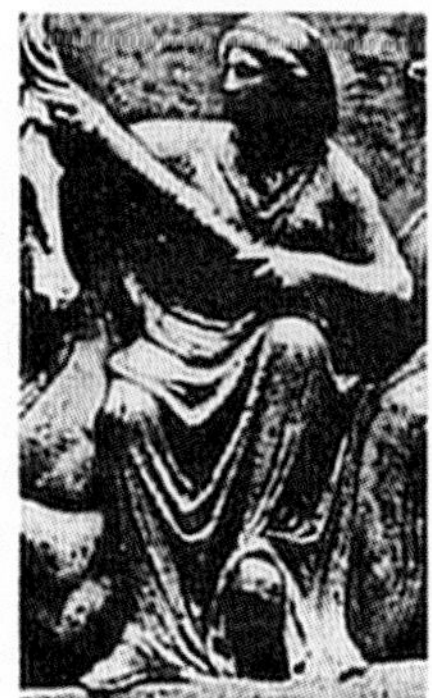

15
Irst century BOT
Roman woman
Relief frieze
Rome

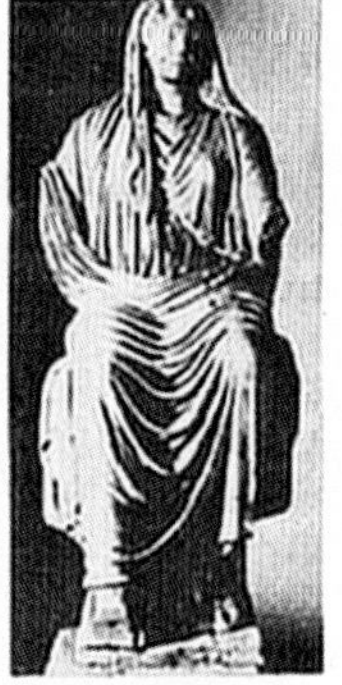

16
Irst century BOT
Statue of Livia,
Paestum

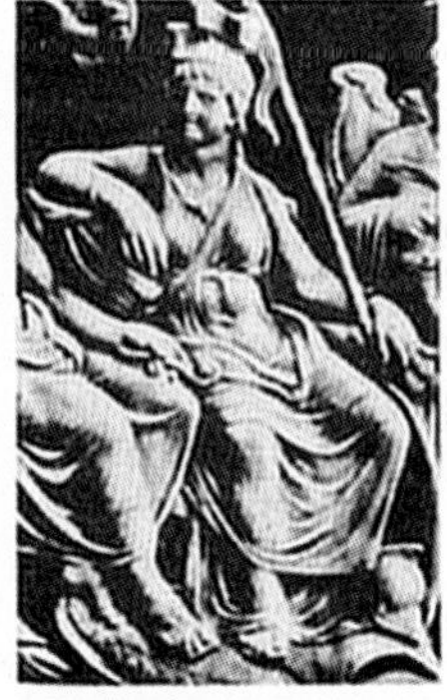

17.
Irst century IOT
Roman woman
Arrival of Tiberius
before Augustus

serious attention again. Wex's book is long out of print and the original panels had been in storage at the Bildwechsel archive of women's art in Hamburg, until a small selection were included in a show which I curated for Focal Point Gallery in Southend in the UK in 2009; the gallery subsequently published a small catalogue, with reproductions from the original book and newly commissioned essays.

The strip-mining of 'lost' artists of the 1960s and 1970s has become a small industry. The most telling example is perhaps Lee Lozano, who made 'dropping out' of the art world into a self-cancelling performance at the time, but whose work has undergone spectacular reappraisal ('one of the least known great artists of the New York scene', as a recent Hauser & Wirth press release put it). But simple acts of restitution and revaluation, however merited, risk papering over the fissures into which those artists' careers had fallen in the first place – not least because, in many cases, those fissures remain. The slight returns which are now such a feature of contemporary art's relationship to its past should not fool us into forgetting the gaps, lapses, occlusions and omissions which necessitated these returns in the first place.

Similarly, if individual artworks or bodies of work are 'orphaned' by artists' later life choices, then they pass down to us with a set of perplexingly familiar but intractable questions: about life and work, intention and history. What, for example, would Hare or Wex's images look like considered instead as part of a life practice, a continuum with what they chose to do since they stopped making them? Are artists really, ultimately, responsible for their own reputations? And are we any better equipped now than thirty years ago to answer what it really means to have a career in art – or, for that matter, to abandon one?

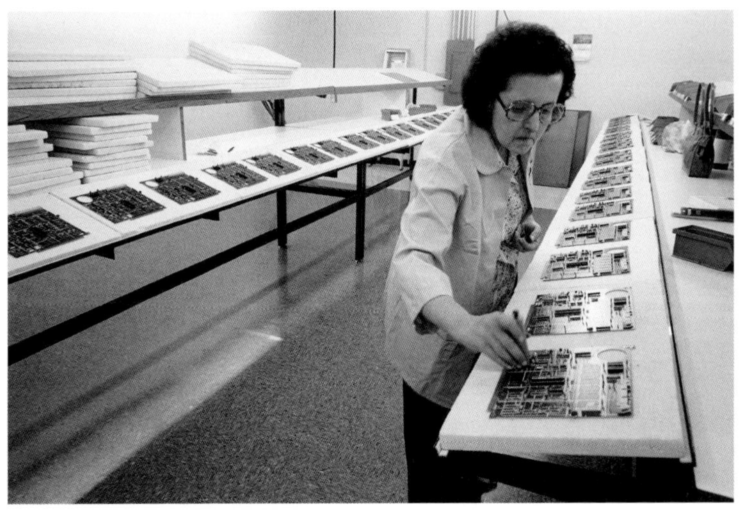

Chauncey Hare, *Woman working in the electronics industry,* 1980/81

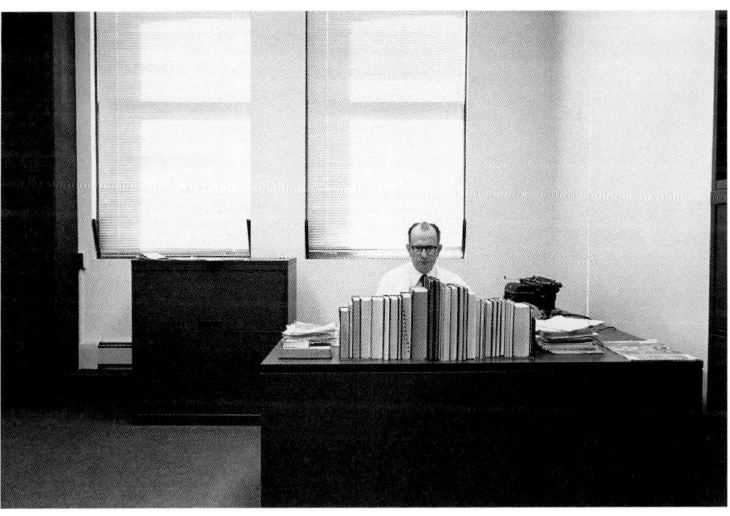

Chauncey Hare, *Office worker seated at a desk behind books, Standard Oil Company of California,* 1976/77

Endnotes

1 Iain Sinclair, *Lights Out For The Territory*, London: Granta, 1997, p. 154.

2 Chauncey Hare, *Protest Photographs*, Göttingen: Steidl, 2009, p. 369.

3 See in this publication, footnote 2, p. 67.

4 Hare, *Protest Photographs*, p. 372.

5 Ibid., p. 16.

6 Ibid., p. 20.

7 Ibid., p. 14.

8 Ibid., p. 16.

9 Marianne Wex, *'Let's Take Back Our Space': 'Female' and 'Male' Body Language as a Result of Partriarchal Structures*, tr. Johanna Albert with Susan Schultz, Hamburg: Frauenliteraturverlag Hermine Fees, 1979, p. 10.

10 Hare, *Protest Photographs*, p. 20.

11 Interview with the author, August 2009. Audio of the interview is available at https://www.fpg.org.uk/exhibition/lets-take-back-our-space (accessed June 1, 2022).

12 Wex, *'Let's Take Back Our Space'*, p. 350.

13 Therapy remains permissible, of course, when clearly introduced and neutralised as subject matter.

14 Janet Malcolm, 'Slouching Towards Bethlehem, PA', *New Yorker*, Aug 6, 1979, p. 80.

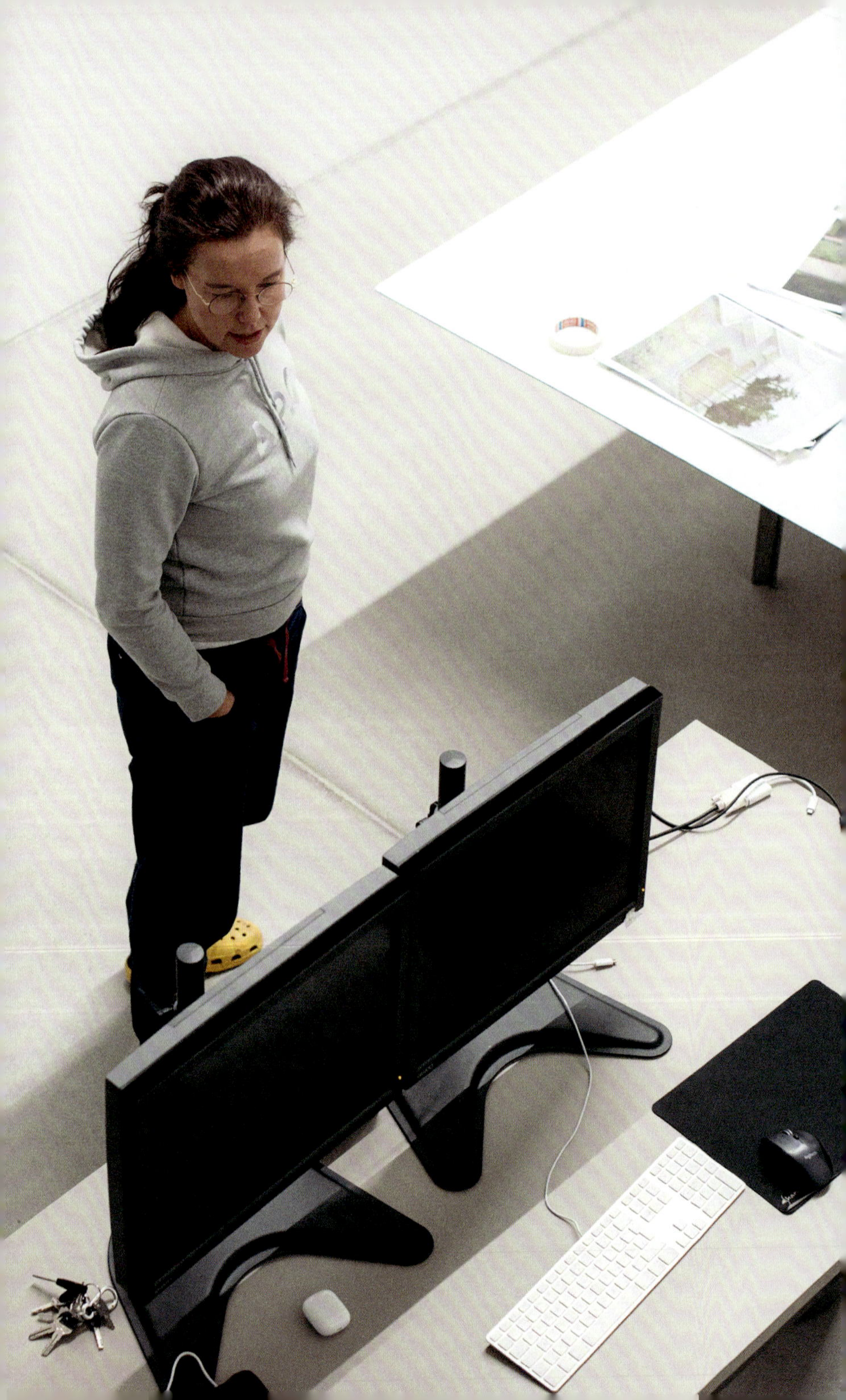

Beate Gütschow, Berlin 2021

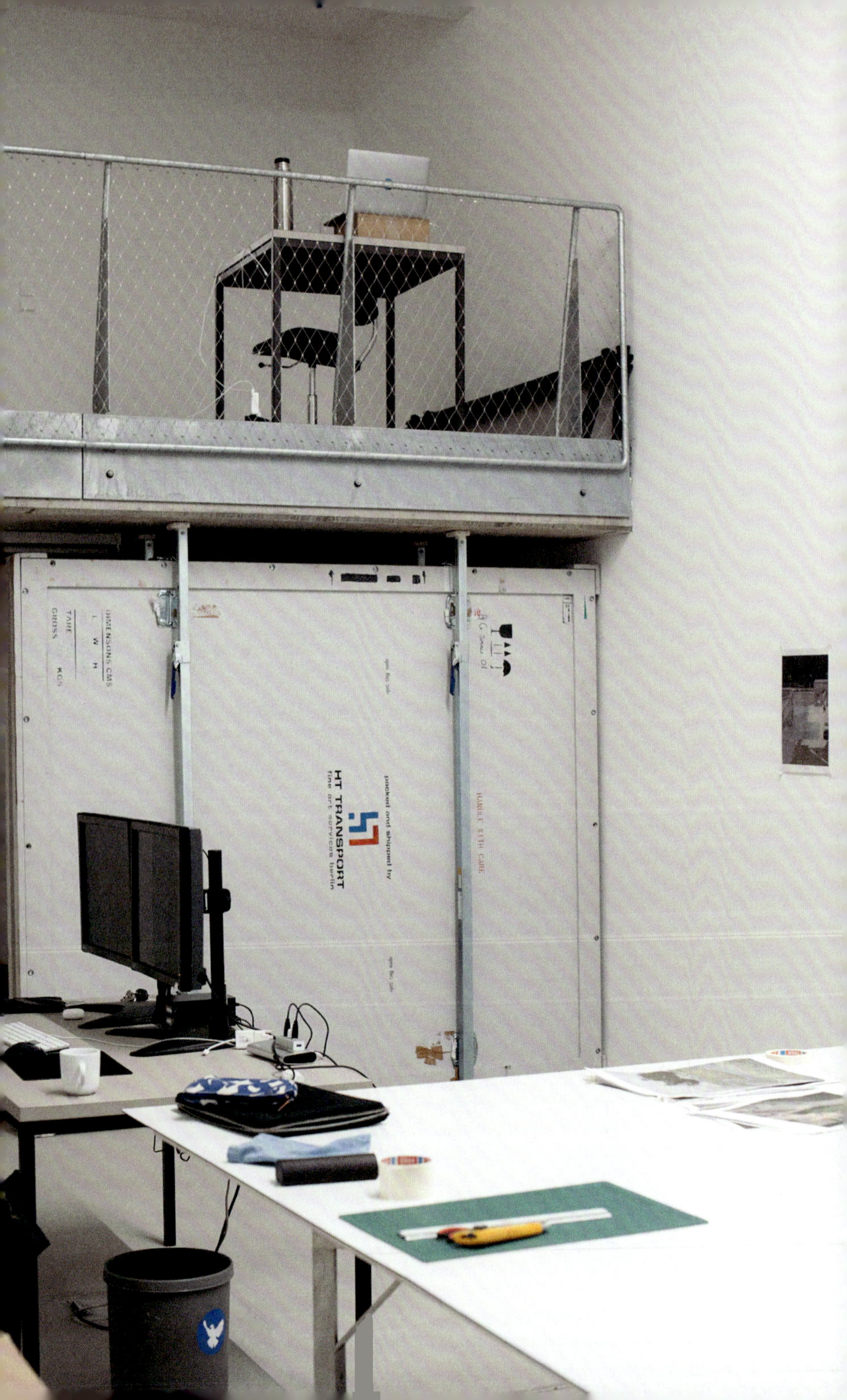
packed and shipped by
HT TRANSPORT
fine art services berlin
DIMENSIONS CMS
L W H
TARE
GROSS
KGS

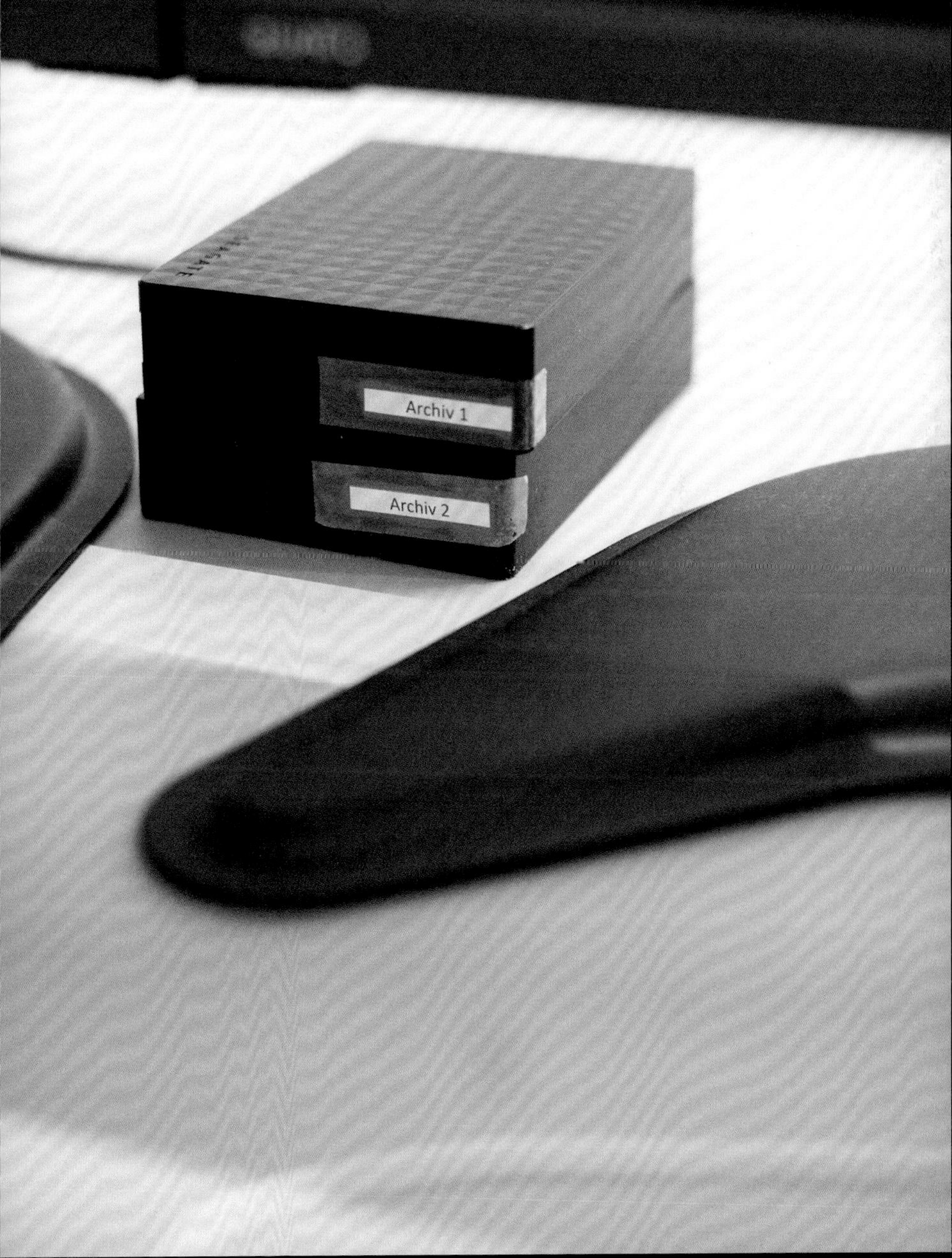
Archiv 1
Archiv 2

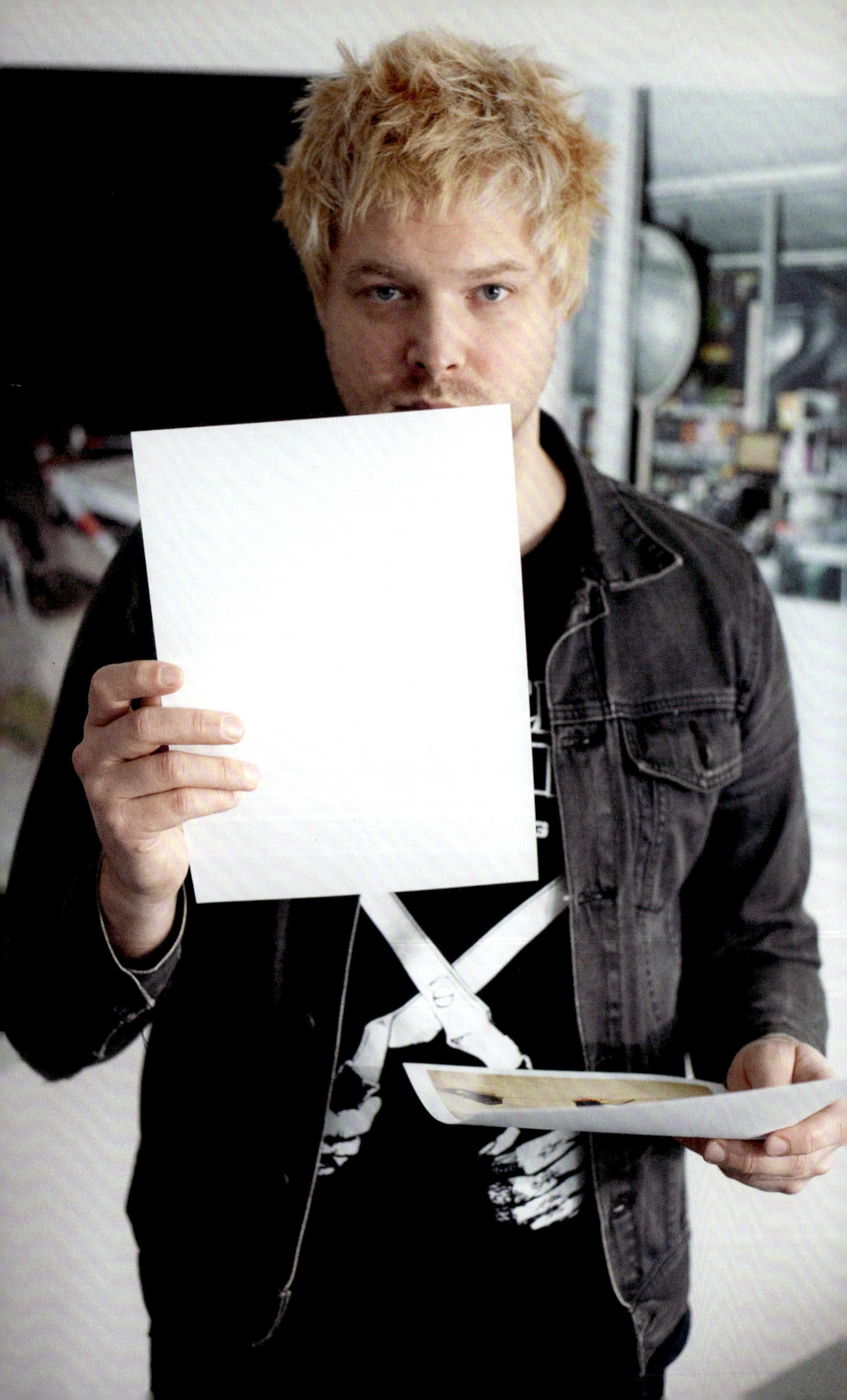

Andreas Langfeld, Berlin 2021

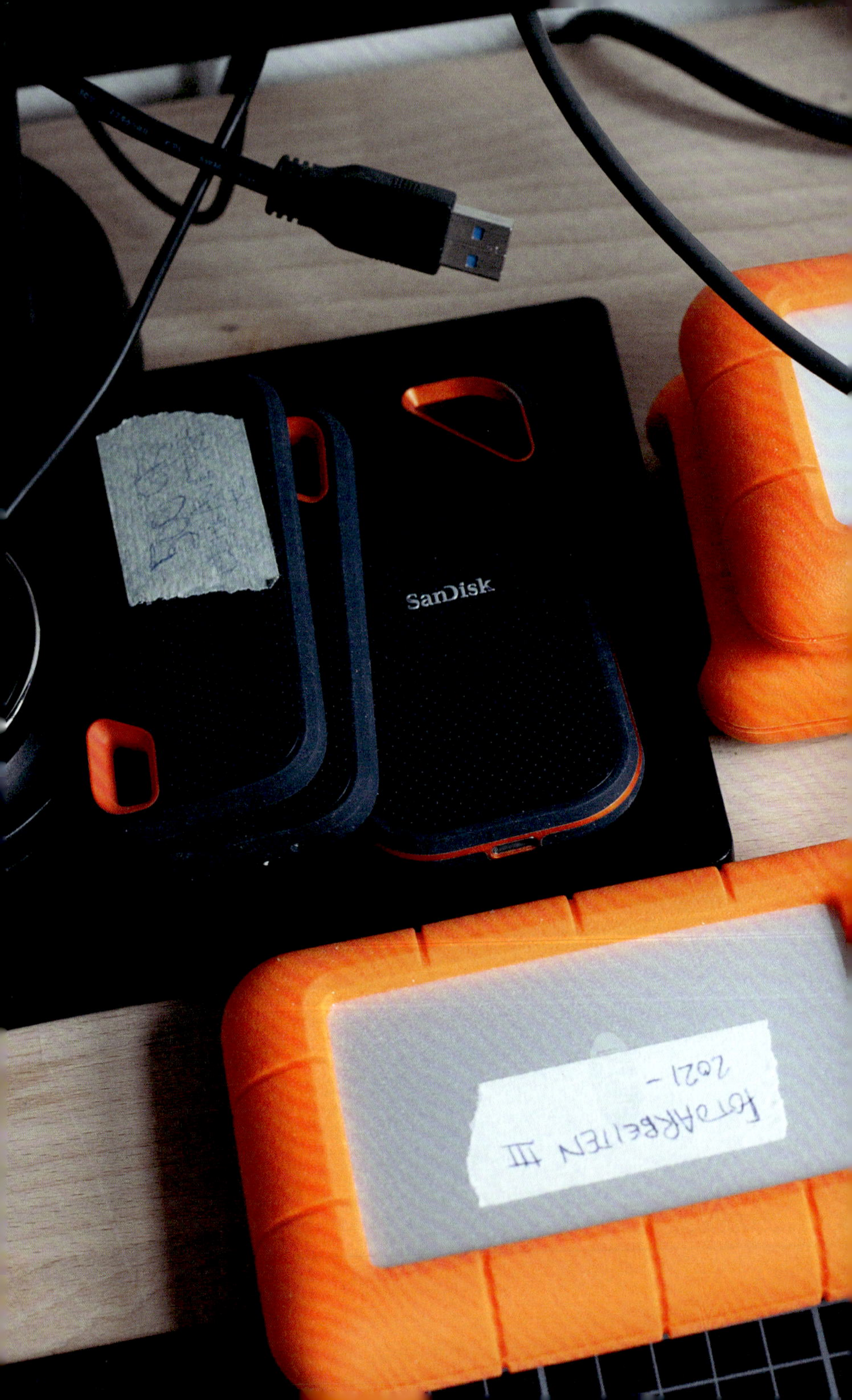
SanDisk
FOTOARBEITEN III
2021 -

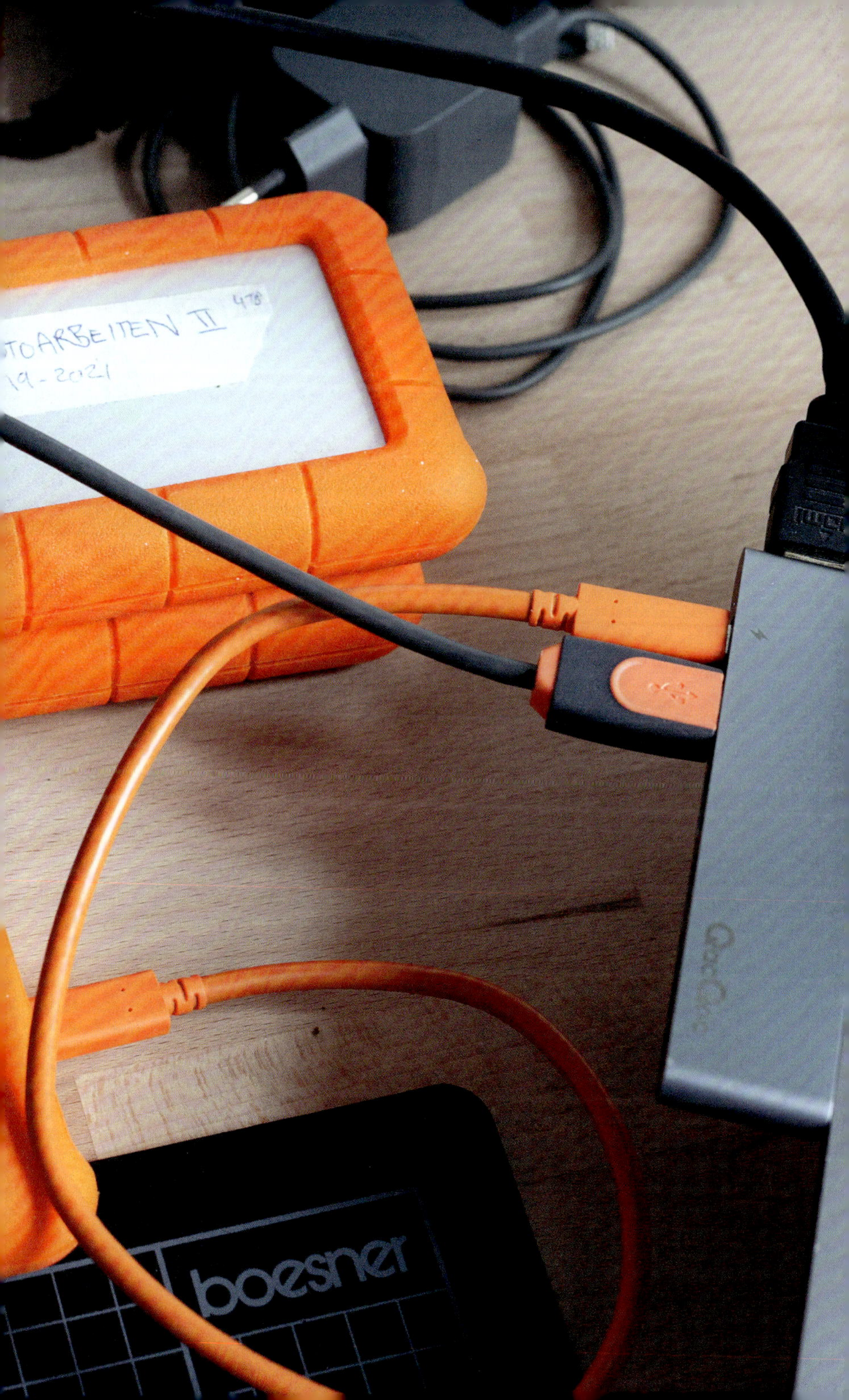
478
TOARBEITEN II
19-2021
boesner

OBJECTS IN TIME

Maren Lübbke-Tidow and
Rebecca Wilton / Lighting the Archive

in conversation with
Mike Sperlinger

Lighting the Archive In your essay 'Two Slight Returns', you write about German artist Marianne Wex and American photographer Chauncey Hare, about their artistic development, and about how their work was treated after the self-imposed end of their careers. When did you first encounter these artists and what was your personal interest in their work?

Mike Sperlinger It's a bit lopsided because I had quite a long, sustained engagement with Marianne Wex's work. Chauncey Hare is someone I was very interested in too, but I only really wrote one text about him. I never had any contact with him and I didn't do a lot of research around his work beyond the available publications.

LTA And when did you first come across Marianne Wex's work?

MS Like 99% of people who know her work, it was through the book version of *Let's Take Back Our Space,* published in 1979. In the early 2000s, a good friend of mine, the filmmaker and photo book collector Matthew Killip, found a copy secondhand and showed it to me. A couple of years later I was asked to do an exhibition for Focal Point Gallery in Southend, London. I thought of this book and wondered what the original materials that formed the book had been and if they still existed. And I couldn't find very much except this website for someone called Marianne Wex, but it didn't say anything about artwork, only about healing practices. So I contacted her to ask if she was the same person and she was. We immediately got into a dialogue about the project. It turned out the materials did exist, in this archive in Hamburg called Bildwechsel, an organisation for women artists, and they'd been storing the material for twenty, twenty-five years at that point. The first time I met Marianne in person would have been in 2008 or 2009.

LTA Was she surprised that someone, especially someone from another country, was interested in her work after all these years?

MS Small venues in Germany had shown some of the panels, but at that point her life was very centred on her healing practice. I don't think she'd been expecting it. But yes, she was excited. Over the years that we worked together, particularly later when we did the show at Badischer Kunstverein in 2012, she became more invested in revisiting that material.

LTA So it became important again for her to work on these materials.

MS Yes. She was already in her seventies by that point, but she was an incredibly energetic person. She really threw herself into it and involved herself very much in installing the show in Southend and then particularly the show at Badischer Kunstverein, where we tried to do something with all of the panels – it was quite hard physical work, even just sorting the panels and organizing them, to try and understand what was there, what the materials really were. We'd only taken a small selection for the Southend show, but there were over 200 panels. She was incredibly energised by the process and started to incorporate some of the thinking and the images back into her healing practice.

LTA It's interesting that for so many years, both for feminist art history and for those interested in photo books, the only point of reference for Marianne Wex's work was this book. But until you contacted her, no one had ever asked: What does the original material look like and where is it? Can something be done with it? So, what kind of shape was the original material in? Because you just mentioned that it was heavy work to install the panels. How had the materials been stored?

MS Maybe the first thing that's important to say is – and I allude to it in my essay in terms of this sort of strip-mining of 'lost' artists that was happening – it tends to come with these heroic narratives of rediscovery. There were definitely moments when I was cast, or even cast myself, in that role in relation to Marianne's work and I really regret that. I think it's very important to reflect that there's a complex trajectory from relative obscurity to being in the MoMA collection as of two years ago (2020). I certainly had a role to play in that, but I think there's lots of other people who were essential, from Matthew Killip showing me the book to all the people at Focal Point Gallery, and above all Anja Casser from Badischer Kunstverein, who co-curated that show with me and really made it possible in the first place. There's also Ruth Buchanan and Andreas Müller, who designed this incredible, iconic exhibition architecture for the Kunstverein, which again had a huge influence on the renewal of interest in Marianne's work – not just in terms of the show itself, but also in the way the images from that show were then disseminated.

LTA Had any restoration been done? Was it in good shape?

MS The narrative tends to be that the work was languishing in an archive and so on. But in a sense, even if they weren't doing active restoration work, this work only existed because Bildwechsel had stored it. What doesn't exist, sadly, are Marianne's paintings. I've done some research to try and find them. There are images – small, poor-quality black-and-white reproductions in her book. But she had this career as a painter in the late sixties doing what look to me like really extraordinary Pop art paintings, often of commercial packaging. They didn't go into the archive, but were either sold or she kept them herself. I think the narrative was that they were stored with a family member while she was travelling the world in the eighties, and at some point they were thrown out or otherwise damaged or destroyed. Nobody has yet traced any of those paintings and they're just gone. Again, for me, it's important with all these narratives about the way things re-enter art history, an institutional history, that we don't over-individualise the agency of how that happens.

The other thing that's important to say in terms of condition is that, thanks to Bildwechsel, the panels were in relatively good shape. I don't know exactly how they were originally displayed, but at some point while travelling to exhibitions in the eighties Marianne arranged to have these plastic sleeves made for them, with rivets they could be hung from. So the original card photocollage panels were protected. These probably weren't ideal conditions, I don't know whether the plastic is archive friendly, but that at least did a certain amount to protect them. What really struck me when I first met Marianne in the archive was that, as well as these panels in the plastic sleeves, we also found cut-up pieces of panels. So there were half panels, bits and pieces where one image had been cut out by Marianne herself, because at some point she decided she needed to reconfigure a panel, or she needed to emphasise something using an image removed from another panel. She was no expert on conservation, there was no preciousness about these objects. They were really objects of use for her, in the early eighties at least. They were well preserved, all things considered, but there was also something very unprecious about the way she treated them.

LTA Today, Marianne Wex's work is represented by Tanya Leighton Gallery in Berlin. You mentioned that some of the panels are now in the collection of the Museum of Modern Art in New York. There's also a panel in the Sammlung Verbund in Vienna. Do you have any information about who bought the panels or whether German institutions were interesting in buying them?

MS It's important to clarify this, because all of the original panels are at MoMA. Around the time of the show at Badischer Kunstverein, I'd been concerned about finding an institutional home for them. That was partly for conservation reasons, because they're panels with printed text and photographs glued to card and they've not been kept in archival conditions. In the long term, there were clearly conservation issues. It was obvious that they hadn't entered institutional art history, although as you said the book had been and was still being referred to, particularly by photobook historians. But the panels didn't have any real presence in art history beyond the reviews that were starting to appear around these new shows. Things often don't really enter art history without entering institutional collections. And I also wanted this to happen before Marianne died because I felt, again, one of the repeated tropes is institutions waiting for artists to die in order to hoover up works that retroactively become important. So I'd been actively trying to find institutions that would do that. Anja Casser, too, was actively contacting German institutions.

I remember at the time she thought there was some interest, but nothing materialised. At a certain point I realised we probably needed to try via the commercial gallery system. Fortunately I was able to approach Tanya Leighton, and she then took on all the original panels and stored them in Berlin, and we did this exhibition in her gallery in 2018. Tanya took on Marianne as one of her artists and she was the one who made the sale of the original panels to MoMA, so she is central to this story too. But before that she also made an edition with Marianne, reproductions of a set of the core panels. So anything that's in a collection other than MoMA is some kind of a later edition. I think there was also an edition that Marianne made some years before the one for Badischer Kunstverein.

LTA Tanya Leighton didn't make these editions from the original negatives, which have been lost, right? So there must have been a process of re-photographing the original panels.

MS Yes, exactly. That's one of the sad things: Marianne had none of the negatives, they were all gone. Which also meant that any new edition of the book would have to be a facsimile of the original edition, because all of the original photographic materials that she made – she herself re-photographed the panels in order to make the book – were also gone.

LTA The response to the exhibition at Tanya Leighton a couple of years ago was enormous. More people than ever before were suddenly writing about her work, which is quite remarkable because, for example, after the appearance of Judith Butler's *Gender Trouble* in 1990, this binary system, which Marianne established in her work, was no longer discussed in feminist theory or by all the people who had previously been referring to Marianne's work. But the show at Tanya Leighton was also interesting in the way it gave an impression of Germany in the seventies and eighties, this post-war situation and what people looked like, how people dressed, and so on. So it's good to have a new edition because that allows German institutions to include it in their collections.

MS This is where you get to the limits of intentionality. I think your point about the change in discussions around gender is really interesting. Marianne's work, for me, tests such gender binaries to destruction. It's about the idea that these are stereotyped roles that are forms of social reproduction, but they're not essences.

LTA Especially when you think of a young generation that is restaging these specific gestures – it's already already this game of gender.

MS The book has this incredibly polemical title and it's always been contextualised in terms of second-wave feminism. I think particularly when second-wave feminism was very out of fashion in the eighties, nineties, the work was just invisible, it was a curio. But what becomes evident when you see the original panels is that this is actually a multifaceted work, with other dimensions including an ethnography of Germany in the mid-seventies. You also have aspects of re-photography, there are reproductions of images appropriated from other books. And there's this kind of Pop art element to it too. It contains within it very different kinds of photographic image – collaged images from magazines, re-photographed history books, street photography – and in that sense it's a conceptual work. The book deliberately has this flattening effect, because it constantly points towards body language and seems to downplay other aspects of these images. But there's also a self-awareness in that gesture. For example, you have an image of a Nazi officer standing on piles of bodies and she cropped it in such a way that you're supposed to just look at the officer's body language, but that's clearly impossible. These images beg the question of what it means to crop and to make your vision so selective that you only see this one thing.

LTA What about Chauncey Hare? Photographer, writer, and theorist Allan Sekula once mentioned his work in his highly influential essay 'Dismantling Modernism' (1978) and then for many years nobody wrote about him, even though there's quite an engaged community around Allan Sekula, but those people also took no notice of him. So how did you encounter Hare's work?

MS It was a complete accident. While I was on the Whitney Independent Study Program in 2006/07, I was researching for the

exhibition we were doing, I think it was at Columbia University Library, going through the art history books. I came across this book *Interior America* from 1978, which I think is his first one. When Steidl reissued them they made this new *Protest Photographs* compilation, but originally the first volume was just called *Interior America*. It showed these photographs of people in their homes, shot with a wide-angle lens. I just thought they were incredible, I'd never seen images like that. When I read about him, I was fascinated that he'd had such a strange career. He seemed to have made this very iconic photobook in the seventies and followed it up with *This Was Corporate America* in 1984 and then suddenly a few years later he had ended up as a therapist working with workplace abuse and completely abandoned photography. And then you start to read about him picketing his own shows, for example, at San Francisco Museum of Modern Art.
On a superficial level I got interested in this parallel with Marianne, especially with *This Was Corporate America* and what he did afterwards. I'm not sure whether I still believe this, but my projection onto both of them was that they didn't simply stop making work, but that the impulses that drove them to make art in the first place eventually drove them to stop making it. The same impulse that made them create these images eventually forced them to move beyond that, to work in other ways through forms of therapy or healing, probably because the institutional art world could not fulfil the aspirations they had for their projects. But although Chauncey Hare would talk about his project as sympathetic, there was also a kind of ruthlessness about it, just as Marianne was ruthless in her cropping. Hare was taking these images with wide-angle lenses where people clearly felt they were being photographed, when really he was much more interested in their peripheries and in seeing the interiors of their homes. There was a kind of typology at work, a taxonomic impulse, but a political or polemical one.

LTA When you were researching Chauncey Hare, your research was based on his artist books? You didn't have the chance to visit the Bancroft Library, for example?[1]

1 Chauncey Hare donated his entire photographic archive to the Bancroft Library, University of California in Berkeley, in 2000.

MS No, I actually didn't. I had a background interest in Chauncey Hare, in comparison to Marianne. I'd been interested in his work for a while and I was excited when the new book came out. That was the impetus for writing this article. Especially after the show at Le Bal in 2010, when it was clear that his images were circulating again.

LTA Do you know if it's easy to get the images for an exhibition? Of course, they have to be exhibited with the specific remark by Chauncey Hare,[2] but is it difficult to get the originals? There was the group show at Le Bal, but these photographs have never been exhibited in Europe before or since.

MS It's true. I was actually waiting for a big solo show and it never happened. Even from the introduction to the Steidl book, it's clear that he was difficult to work with and imposed a lot of restrictions. But I don't know, I never tried.

LTA In the last part of your essay you speak about work by forgotten artists being discovered and what could be problematic about this. How important do you think it is to include biographical facts in relation to an artist's work? For example, when you're doing a posthumous show and you're not able to involve the artist personally. How much biographical information do we need? How important was it for you, for example, when discovering Marianne Wex's work to learn about her life and, ultimately, to meet her in person?

MS It was very important for me to meet Marianne. I would say three aspects of my life or career have affected my thinking about this question in different ways. One was working for more than ten years at LUX, an archive of artist's films in London, and dealing with issues around artists who had disappeared,

2 'For social situation photographs (1967 to 1985) the following text must accompany each publication or exhibition presentation of one or more of Chauncey Hare's photographs: "These photographs were (or 'this photograph was') made by Chauncey Hare to protest and warn against the growing domination of working people by multi-national corporations and their elite owners and managers."' See https://oac.cdlib.org/findaid/ark:/13030/k6pn966r/entire_text.

making it impossible for us to trace whose work we held, or other artists who had very active or overactive estates, with very strong opinions about how the work should be shown. I was navigating those things from the perspective of an institution, albeit a small one.

The second was meeting Marianne. I think at the time when I first met her, I was much less interested in questions of the artist's biography or even intentionality. That was not so important to me, which was maybe also the product of having come to art via philosophy and especially Adorno. But the process of working with Marianne for ten years shifted that for me profoundly.

And the third thing was my close friendship and working relationship with Ian White, the artist, writer, and curator. When he died in 2013, I was involved in running his estate, together with Josephine Pryde. That forced me to inhabit some of those questions in a very different way, for example when I was working on an exhibition of his work at Camden Art Centre in 2018 with Kirsty Bell. Ian is important for thinking about this, because for him, artworks of all kinds – he worked particularly as a curator with film – can never just be, as it were, dug out of an archive and exhibited. Every act of exhibition is an act of performance, the work has to perform. And in that sense it's a fantasy that the works are autonomous, that they carry all of this meaning with them, and that they can be self-sufficient and so on. This is true even with paintings, I think, but particularly with other works, where the boundary between the work and the context is much more porous.

LTA Practices of performance raise many questions about how to convey a work, of course. An artist like Ian White seemed to unify these questions in his work, precisely because he himself worked a lot with performances, in addition to many other art forms.

MS I'd like to stress an idea I spoke about with Ian just before he died, when we were talking about how to deal with the afterlife of his works. He talked about everything that he'd done and called them 'objects in time'. That meant that they were going to keep ageing and being transformed, even if, as it were, they were just sitting in an archive somewhere and were physically the same. They were always going to be transformed by historical change around them. And they were going to need to be re-performed and re-interpreted. Which again was part of his philosophy about all works, that even if they seemed to have been constant over hundreds of years, like Renaissance masterpieces, somehow that's never the case, they always need to be re-instantiated. In that sense, I think we need this expanded sense of what the work is, that includes perhaps the artist's life and intentionality, but also the history of the work, all the things that happened to it between the moment of its creation and the moment when we're seeing it.

It might be about questions of biography, but it might also simply be a question of understanding an artwork as one gesture in a series of gestures. For example, thinking about Marianne's encyclopaedic project as just one gesture among others that she made over the course of her life, as part of a larger trajectory which was about something else, about more than just body language. And if you read the autobiographical text at the end of the book, I think it's one of the most clear-sighted texts by an artist exploring the evolution of their own work that I've ever read. To understand how her interest in Pop art and packaging turns into an interest in photography and body language, and then basically by the end an interest in commodification – commodification of the body, but also commodification of everyday life. And then she moves into self-healing. I think all this is important to understanding the project and in that sense there's a real question about how to present the work, in both curatorial and archival terms.

One of the things that was important for me in working with Marianne to find an institutional home for the work was to preserve its conceptual core along with the materials. After I had travelled to meet her for an interview, we made this protocol for the work together and I believe it was used at least at some point in the MoMA sale. Marianne herself talked about ways in which her images had, at certain moments when she was first exhibiting them, been displayed in touring shows in ways that were completely contrary to what she had intended. For example, she mentioned a show where all of the female images had been hung in one room and the male images in another.

Let's Take Back Our Space was actually a very conceptual work. There was almost a kind of algorithmic logic for thinking about how it worked. When working on exhibitions, she was very responsive to context. If it was a group show, she would select the panels in a slightly different way to respond to other works in the show and so on. So I wanted to find a way to codify this. One temptation might be, for example, once those works are archived, to take them out of their sleeves and put them in frames. But as soon as the works are framed, they start to become more singular, iconic images. Whereas for me, and I think for Marianne too, this is a work that's about a *system*, it's a serial work. That's something important to preserve. There's no way of doing that without text, without some kind of protocol to accompany the work.

LTA Some of the examples you're giving are less about the artist's biography and more about material context, aren't they? The notes in *Let's Take Back Our Space* are more about controlling how the work should be shown. Having information about how to show works is important. The question of 'mythologisation' may play a part here, but in the cases of Chauncey Hare and Marianne Wex don't we really need to know about the artist's biography since they decided to stop making art and started doing something completely different instead? And doesn't the same apply, for example, to minoritised artists – like those who worked in the former GDR? For many years these works were considered less important because they didn't match the Western canon. The artists were not able to work freely, they were required to follow specific 'guidelines'. Now we are slowly realizing that they made important art under a repressive regime and that it's important, in this case, to know about the artist's biography. Instead of putting up an artwork on the gallery wall and giving the honour that belongs to the work, it's also important to mention what happened to the artist and why she or he was working on these pieces. Like what you meant with the fissures of an artist's life.
There was an important curator in the 1990s in Berlin, Frank Wagner, who died in 2016. He made an exhibition series called *Unterbrochene Karrieren* (Interrupted Careers), and he included artists like Hannah Wilke or Joe Spence, who at a certain point in their lives had a cut in their careers, whether because

they became ill, were subjected to repression, or simply decided to quit their job as artists for whatever reason. Of course, that doesn't correspond to the way we've learnt to think about artists' work. Our way of looking at art in the Western canon is very much split up.
Because you've been working with so many artists who maybe are more in these 'artist's artist' spheres or even minoritised, for example when we are thinking about the history of LUX, then it might be interesting to look more precisely at the artist's biography.

MS Absolutely. I'm still resisting the word biography. Biography and intentionality are certainly important, in ways that perhaps, working from certain traditions, we have not recognised until more recently. Understanding artworks not as sealed monads that are released into the world and generate their meaning autonomously, but as always part of a series of gestures that, for example, constitute a life. I often think of a text Andrea Fraser wrote in the nineties about conceptual artworks that tried to perform a critique of the market, which concludes by saying: we can't talk about the politics of art simply through the things that people make, we have to examine them in relation to the positions that artists take. There's a certain kind of artwork, at least, which just doesn't have these fixed boundaries, it doesn't have a clear frame. The frame is always going to be re-instantiated every time it's shown. That frame is about a kind of context. And that context might be about the artist's life, but it might also be about the context in which that life was lived and the forms of resistance that it involved.
Recently I was teaching around writing by Lorraine O'Grady, who was part of the Guerrilla Girls, an artist I think of as another interesting parallel to Marianne Wex in many ways. She worked partly with photocollage and made some strikingly similar works to Marianne, looking at the relationship between portrait photographs and statuary and so on. She's a brilliant writer, too, and her work is very informed by being a Black artist working, for long periods, on the margins of the American art world. But she also really complicates that, as when she talks about the idea of making work that is 'counter-confessional'. She talks about making a work using *New York Times*

headlines as a kind of autobiography that's done outside-in, like when you're talking about your life through these things that are meeting you from the outside. That to me is a more interesting image of what thinking about biography might mean. It's not, for example, necessarily about tracing intentionality back to some source of interiority, but more about reconstructing the conditions under which a certain gesture was necessary and possible, or even impossible.

LTA That might also link to the end of your essay where you're talking about the fissures?

MS What I was trying to get back to – in a somewhat self-aware way in relation to my own work with Marianne Wex – was the idea that there's a kind of affirmation that seems to come automatically with these acts of restitution. It's perceived as an act of restitution and recovery. These are all very positive-sounding terms that are, in a sense, about righting a wrong. Whereas, in a way, the historical meaning of that work is connected to the blockages that it encountered in the first place. If you simply restitute, you lose part of the meaning of the work, which is that it was made in the face of all this resistance, and that somehow you have to bring the resistance along with the work. Otherwise, if the resistance is completely invisible, the work risks becoming meaningless through its apparent self-evidence – when twenty or thirty years ago it couldn't even be shown, because there was so much resistance. You somehow have to bring that context, that resistance with you. Otherwise it's institutional or curatorial narcissism, simply a form of self-celebration. And we know that, in an extremely basic kind of capitalist logic, the art world loves nothing more than finding ways to re-valorise its own fiercest critics, at a safe enough remove. It's the risk of these acts that you need to bring with them, in any act of restitution – if that's what it is, it needs to also restitute the friction or the gaps. Pointing to biography is perhaps one way of doing that, by saying: what we are showing here now could not be, or was not, shown in a previous period and this person suffered. That's a way of trying to carry that with the work. But I think there are other ways of doing it. With

Marianne's work, it became important to me to think about her healing work, about which I have to say I was initially quite sceptical. I felt it was a kind of New Age practice that I was not very comfortable with, or perhaps even embarrassed by. But I thought it was important to bring that into relation, particularly because for her this whole body of work was simply a way of thinking. For Marianne this wasn't supposed to be a masterwork that was going to be institutionally framed and preserved. It was in a continuum, a form of thinking that she was pursuing through her healing work. And one form of resistance she encountered is the way the art world is still terrified of these forms – art therapy, for example, is still something that's quite taboo in a way.

LTA But it's changing!

MS That's true.

LTA Maybe Marianne Wex and Chauncey Hare could have devoted their lives to today's art world, where they might have had the chance to include their healing practice into their art practice. You said it doesn't make sense to talk about Marianne Wex's work as a masterpiece, trying to understand it instead as a way of thinking, which is always the best moment in art. But maybe they wouldn't have been forced to make those radical cuts in their lives and start to work as healer or therapist, considering that today this is a major aspect of contemporary art.

MS Yes, I think there's more possibility for that. I may be not quite as optimistic, but I agree. I think there are ways in which there could have been more continuity in their work, in their lives. That reminds me of another example in Marianne's case, when I recorded an interview with her for the Focal Point show. One thing she said very clearly is, 'all art to me is research'. Research-based practice is now, academically at least, among the most affirmed and well supported and funded. But at that point, when her work was first shown in Berlin in 1977, there was a discussion about whether it was even art, whether this was not really 'just' an art history display. They couldn't process the idea of a research project that was an artwork. So certainly, that work would have been received in different ways now than it was then, absolutely.

LTA That's interesting, coming back to the artwork and its context, because in conversations within the Lighting the Archive project we always end up discussing with the artist where the artwork begins and where it ends, and whether there are important things that must be carried next to the artwork. For example, when thinking about archiving it or donating it as a pre-mortem bequest. There are some institutions in Germany that allow artists and authors to hand over their work for archiving. This also links to your work with the Ian White estate, because you had to take decisions about what's included and in which ways, and how to proceed with it. With Ian White and also with Marianne Wex you were fortunate to know these people quite well and discuss these things. Of course, it's different when this isn't possible. What was your approach with Ian White's estate?

MS It's interesting because I was reading the interview you did for *Eikon* magazine,[3] where you talk about how one of the difficulties in discussing these issues with living artists is that it means confronting your own mortality. In that sense, it can be quite profound. With Marianne we would talk about it in those terms, but she was already near her eighties. With Ian it was different, but he was dying of cancer. Some of the conversations happened with the clear understanding that his death was imminent. What was interesting, after he died, was going through his materials and realising it was already archived. From the very first things he'd done, even stuff from school, he'd kept it – not exhaustively catalogued, but it was ordered. In his teens he must already have had a sense of this need to organise and to preserve things he'd done. For example in the 1990s he did a project with Dennis Cooper at the Horse Hospital, a venue in London, and he'd even printed out emails from Cooper, correspondence that otherwise would be long lost. Perhaps this was partly because

3 'In Focus: Lighting the Archive. From the Engine-Room of Art. Maren Lübbke-Tidow, Rebecca Wilton, and Linda Conze in Conversation', in *Eikon – International Magazine for Photography and Media Art,* no. 117/2022, pp. 53–63.

Ian was a queer man in the nineties, working within recent living memory of the AIDS crisis. But regardless, his own mortality was part of his making and thinking almost from the beginning.
I should stress that I wasn't the only one involved in these conversations. Others were also caring for him and thinking about the fate of his work, particularly Josephine Pryde who initially ran the estate with me. So it was always a kind of collective endeavour. I remember that I tried to talk to him quite directly about his performance work, for example, and the idea that other people might perform it, whether that was conceivable. It was difficult for him to talk about. I think if we'd spoken about it two years before he died, it would have been different. To speak about that, in that moment, meant directly confronting his own death. That we were going to live with the task of preserving his work was difficult to talk about.
Basically what he did was to give us parameters. The most important were what he called, somewhat flippantly, 'serving suggestions'. He said it was very important to remove the idea of a single representation of any performance, because he performed most of his performances several times, and they were documented each time. It was important to him that not one of these become iconic or definitive. He insisted on the idea of failure and repetition. He was talking about this on his deathbed – about the way his work would live on, the idea of maintaining its inconsistencies and its multiplicities. He talked about the important thing being the movement between elements, not the static parts. And he said everything he did was a means of being in the world. He connected that to this idea about 'objects in time'. There was an idea of gestures that had a moment and had a meaning in that moment. If they were to be revisited by someone else, it would need to be with a sense of what they meant *now*, in a radical sense – not in an act of historical recovery, or about trying to discover what they had meant to Ian when he did them.
There was something liberating in these parameters he gave us. But when it came to it, when Kirsty Bell and I curated the show at Camden Art Centre, it was actually very challenging to imagine in practice what this meant in a gallery exhibition. I'm not sure whether it was successful, but we tried to restage several works and to think of a different logic of restaging for each one.

For example, with Ian's piece *Democracy* we showed all of the existing video documentation from different iterations of the performance. There were four different monitors playing simultaneously, and you would watch them going in and out of sync, it was about that multiplicity. The work *Trauerspiel* from Berlin we actually showed in a more traditional performance documentation style as a frieze of still photographs. And when it came to the work he did with Jimmy Robert, Jimmy radically restaged elements from projects they'd done together – it became basically a new work. So there was this sense of trying out all these different things and trying definitively not to make anything definitive! We needed to think through in practice what these works meant in our present.

LTA You're running the foundation of Ian White's estate, but you're not keeping everything, right? Have some of the materials already been given to other collections?

MS It's complicated, but the most significant thing so far is that all his working notes have gone to the Center for Curatorial Studies at Bard College. Everything else, more or less, is still with the estate. But although Ian himself was ambivalent about it, I'd like to find an institutional home for some of the work, because I think otherwise, as with Marianne, things don't enter art history. So I'm trying to think about a way to do that which would be responsible and it's difficult. That's an ongoing question. There are lots of practical problems, especially with such a performance-based body of work. I spoke to a few people and one of the most helpful was Lisa Le Feuvre, who recently became director of the Holt/Smithson Foundation. One thing she said was that she understood the foundation's lifespan as being very finite. She wasn't thinking of the foundation as being something that was going to be there forever to preserve the memory of Robert Smithson and Nancy Holt. Her idea was more that it was necessary for perhaps twenty years to work actively to place things in collections or create new contexts of understanding for the work, and that if this work was successful enough it could potentially dissolve itself. For me, that was a very liberating idea.

LTA It's also often the case that foundations run out of money, so it's actually only meant to be for a couple of years, from the outset.

MS That's really pertinent, because the Estate has already run out of money. What was important with Camden was to do an exhibition as a test case – not to fix the work in particular forms as to how they would then be shown in the future, but more to show a set of possibilities for interpretation. I also edited a book of Ian's writings, published in 2016, and made a website for the estate, and we did an online project to launch that with Eleanor Ivory Weber called 'Limit as Material' in 2020. That, again, is a way of at least having information about the work publicly available.
For me, one outstanding question is whether any of the work belongs in an institutional collection. There's this one piece called *Six Years*, which is a work on paper, a collage related to his performance work *Black Flags*. Kirsty Bell and I had it framed for practical reasons for the Camden show, albeit with some reservations. That's a work I can imagine entering a collection. But I'm reluctant to do that, certainly for that work in isolation, because it feels very unrepresentative, like it's a somewhat dead version of his work without other things alongside it. But it's very difficult to turn his performances into protocols that could easily be sold or put into a collection. And it's even harder to think about a recipe for how to show the documentation videos of his performances, in relation to his own ideas about failure and repetition. It's very hard to get institutions to think in terms of failure and repetition, however much you put it into a legal contract! So that's something I'm still really struggling with in terms of trying to put a full stop to this work, which I think has to happen at a certain point. That's the kind of last challenge. I'm very happy that the papers are at Bard, that's a good context for them. The other collections at Bard are really relevant to his practice and I think the people running the library are very interesting, radical, politicised thinkers who understand the context of queer, alternative art practice Ian was engaged in.

LTA As a curator, you're working at two different ends. You're in contact with marginalised artists – by which we don't mean Ian White, who was well known in a specific art scene in the 1990s and 2000s – but also with very established institutions because, as you said before, if you don't get the artists' works into some collections or institutions they won't be inscribed into art history. But how to stay in touch with artists whose works have so much to do with saying 'no' or refusal? This is even a thing in Ian White's practice, like really trying to inhabit the institutions and to always open up the boundaries. How do you stay in contact with artists who work with refusal as a motor, on the one hand, and then, on the other hand, maintain contact with these highly established institutions which have their own way of preserving the works?

MS When I hear myself talk about aspiring to find an institutional home, my thinking about this has actually changed even over that last few years. In terms of artists working with film and video, the MoMA, for example, has historically had a separate film archive collection where works have been acquired on completely different terms and with much less cultural status than in the main collection. So I've been hung up on the idea that – to have these works included in art history – we need to negotiate with these institutions. But I have to say, in the last five years, the direction of the neoliberal institution feels less and less relevant and more and more hollowed out.

And I think we're getting close to the point where we can stop thinking of those as the repositories and nodal points for our history. I hope so. Especially in terms of how to deal with questions of refusal. I think Ian is the archetypal artist of the refusal, of the 'no', his whole practice is. But I'm reminded about this beautiful book by French philosopher Catherine Malabou called *The Ontology of the Accident*. There's a great chapter about whether it's ever possible to say 'no'. The idea that just the act of saying 'no' is already an affirmation of the possibility of saying 'no'. It somehow presupposes a certain positivity that when one says 'no', one affirms the possibility that it's possible to refuse. That's interesting in relation to our role as curators – or archivists, or just allies, associates, friends – of people working in these radically critical ways. How do you preserve that? How do you hold on to the affirmative possibility of refusal without defanging it? And in terms of my essay, this was definitely part of the anxiety underpinning the text about my own role in restituting a practice like Marianne Wex's in a way that covers up the scars that made that practice possible and also made it impossible, in a way, in a certain period of time.

LTA Treating such aspects of refusal or saying 'no' in this way is intrinsic to a specific performative practice, because otherwise you wouldn't be able to enlarge the canon or change the norms of art.

MS This canon question is interesting. For example, I'm doing a project now in Norway, a screening series that originally came out of thinking about what an alternative film culture in Norway might mean. What would it mean from a contemporary perspective? What are the histories of experimental film in Norway? Because they're quite marginal. But I increasingly felt that I didn't want just a new exercise in canon-building. Then I found an amazing quote from this Norwegian filmmaker called Erik Borge from the sixties, where he was talking about how there was a form lacking in Norwegian film culture, what he called the artistic short film. He had another name for it which was 'the deviant product', which he defined as 'the strange, the difficult, the angry'. I felt that was such a beautiful, open definition – the idea of a film that's deviant, that's actually defined only negatively as being the thing that doesn't fit the commercial, industrial system. That felt very helpful to me, and it was liberating. Instead of the need to positivise this counter-canon, let's look more for the gaps, let's look for the things that aren't being supported, affirmed, recognised, and start from that. To me, in this particular moment, it was more hopeful because we've just been through so many cycles now of recuperation of these practices. I'm very interested in early conceptual art and it's so interesting to look at something like Lucy Lippard's *Six years,* and the introduction to that, where she's already talking about the complete failure of the project of so-called dematerialisation and the idea that this was some kind of escape from the market, and that this attempt to institutionally canonise these counter-practices always collapses, at least in the landscape that we inhabit. In our thinking, then, we have to let go of our investment in canons and institutions. In my view, radical disinvestment needs to happen before we can get anywhere.

LTA We were recently talking not about the term deviant but about the necessary presence of some form of dissonance.

MS Dissonance? Absolutely. 'Deviant' is very loaded, but I was trying to find synonyms, and dissonance is definitely one. Concerning the link between your project and this potential museum, the institute for photography, I think there's a big danger with such archival institutions, and perhaps especially in relation to photography. With photography, there's the illusion that you preserve the work by preserving the negative, connected with a fetishisation of the material. Photography is already linked to indexicality and that somehow promises that by preserving the photographic negative, you can then reproduce it into infinity. What's helpful about the Chauncey Hare example is the idea that this simply isn't the case, that there may be practices where the negative remains completely pristine in the archive and yet its historical substance has completely dissolved, its relevance or meaning having disappeared in the meantime. The institutional logic of preserving the material doesn't preserve the historical substance of the work.
I'm kind of curious from your perspective about this project in relation to the museum and whether you have any utopian ideas about what this intervention might do, for example whether it's an intervention in what form such an institution takes? Or is it more about trying to create parallel initiatives, parallel conversations in relationship to that?

LTA Well, first we recognised the lack of the voices of artists themselves, with their profound knowledge of materials and how artists deal with them, and how they probably already have a storage system, or order, or even have nothing at all, never having thought about it. As we expected, of course, the range is endless. How should an institution deal with that? Each institution has standards and a specific order for the preservation and presentation of its collection. The Lighting the Archive project is still ongoing and at the moment we can't even think about an end, because there are still so many different ways of working with photography, and the medium itself changes all the time. It's such a multifaceted question. We're collecting content, that's the idea. But of course, no one involved in planning the institution ever asks us what we're doing. When it comes to the discussion of an institute for photography in Germany, there's often this strange idea that the material stored there would be something like a homogeneous mass. This is a misconception, because the artists we've been interviewing all work in completely different ways and their material requires specific treatment. It's also important to highlight the problem of the need for selection and the question of how to deal with so many artists who have been overlooked or fallen by the wayside. Because artists already established on the art market are the ones the institute probably aims to collect. But these well-known artists already have an archive or even a foundation. We all know artists who are making great work and who never had the chance and will never have the chance to be exhibited in the institutions. What about them? We're not running with the flag: let's put all the marginalised artists into the institution. Because we're not sure what to think of this ideal of an institute of photography, in part due to the exclusive focus on the medium of photography.

MS That misconception does seem odd, in 2022. Benjamin Cook, the director of LUX, was visionary in this respect in that we'd inherited this tradition from the London Filmmakers Coop where essentially anyone who wanted to be in the collection would be in it. They just gave a film print and they could take it away again at any time. The institution didn't own it, but it was a kind of a service and it was open access, which is amazing. That was possible when you only had a certain volume of stuff being made on 16mm for example. But once video was cheaply accessible, it became impossible. So then we had to have selection criteria. What Ben realised was that instead of being so focused on the archives, the organisation has to have all of these different activities like concentric circles, so you can work with many more artists in many different ways, in ways that empower them to do things for themselves, whether it's about archiving or distributing or producing. So the archive is an anchor that gives you credibility with funders, for example, because it seems so tangible. But you don't make that the locus of everything you do, because otherwise, like you say, you have this bottleneck effect and you just invest more in practices that are already institutionally recognised.

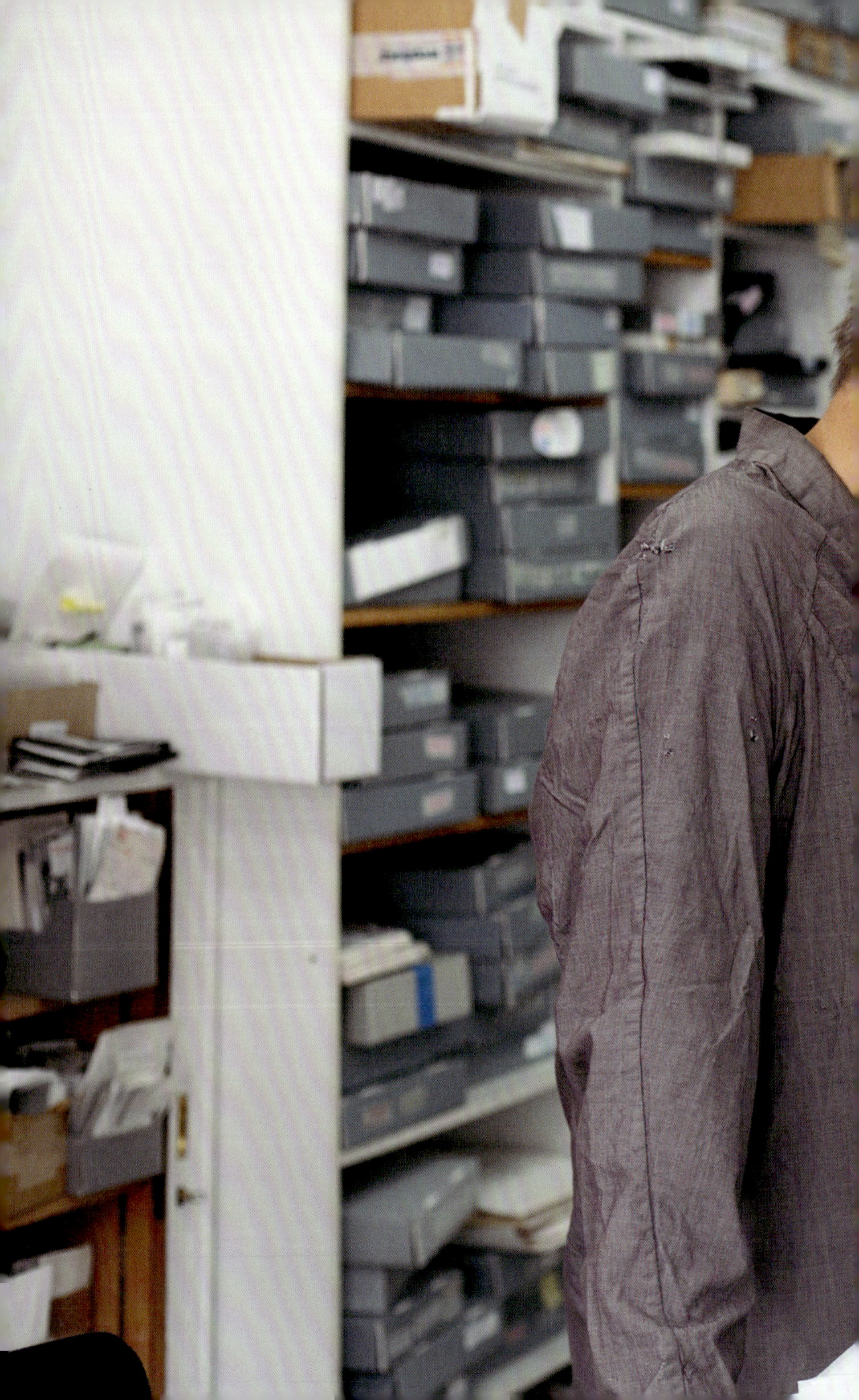

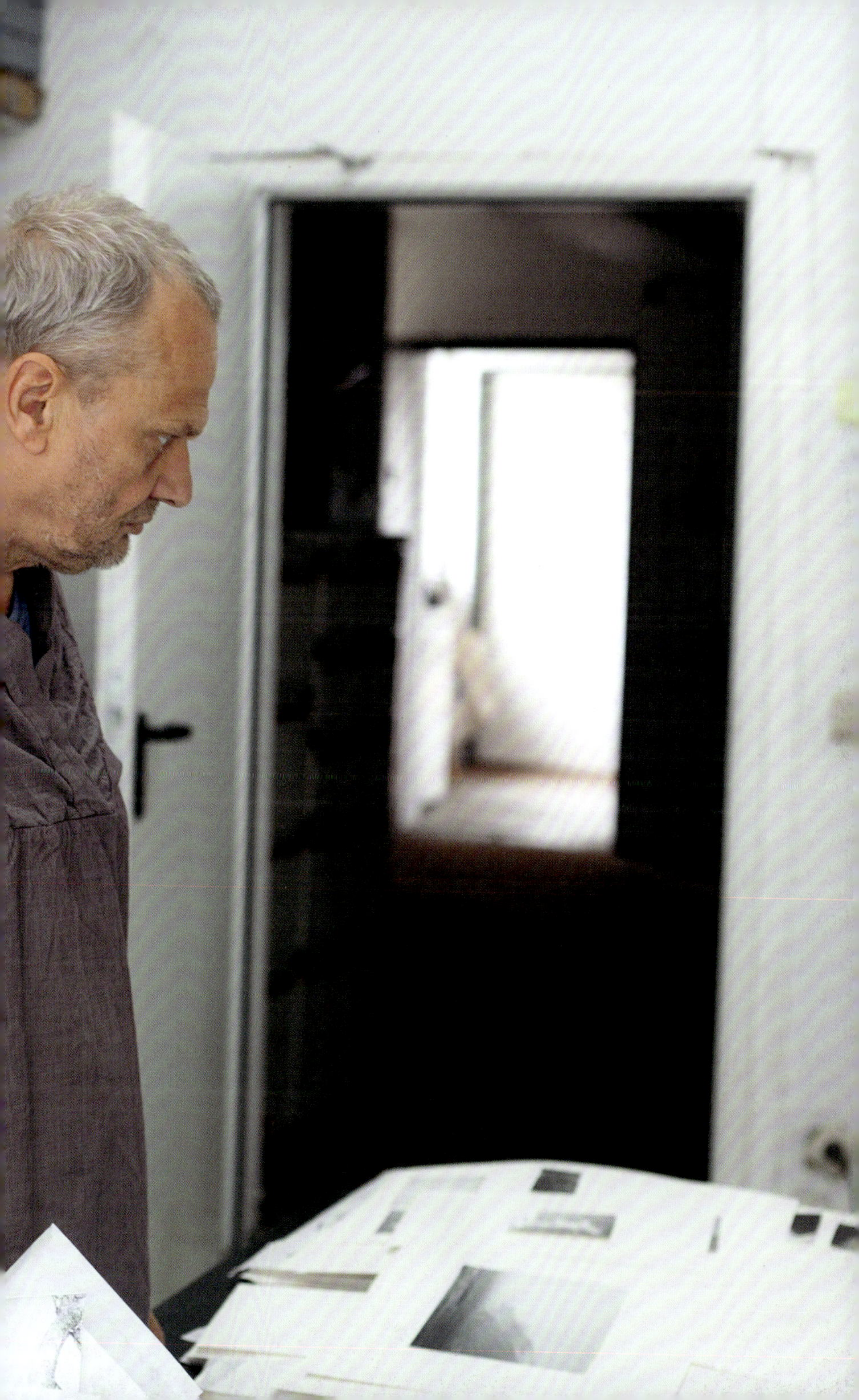

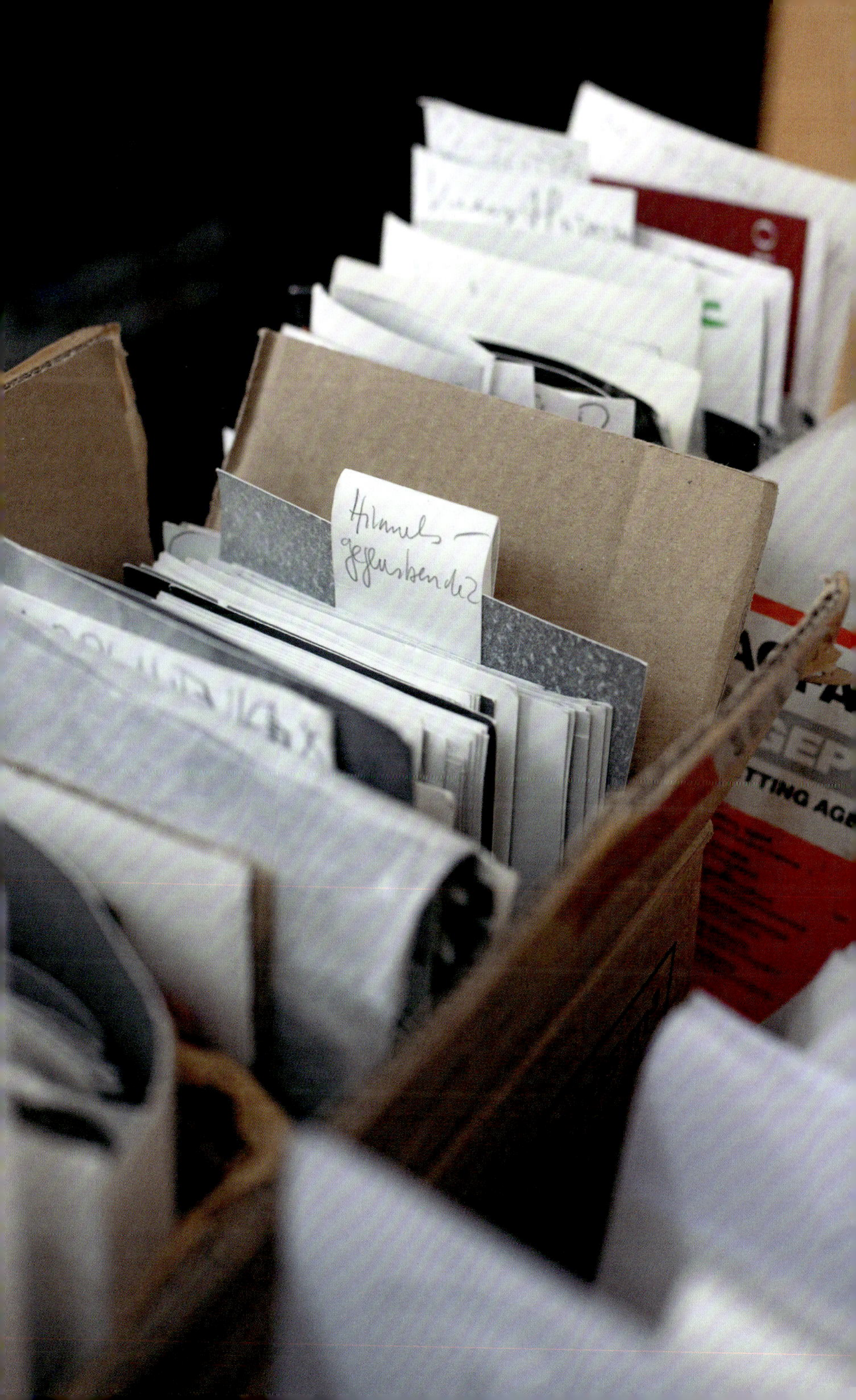

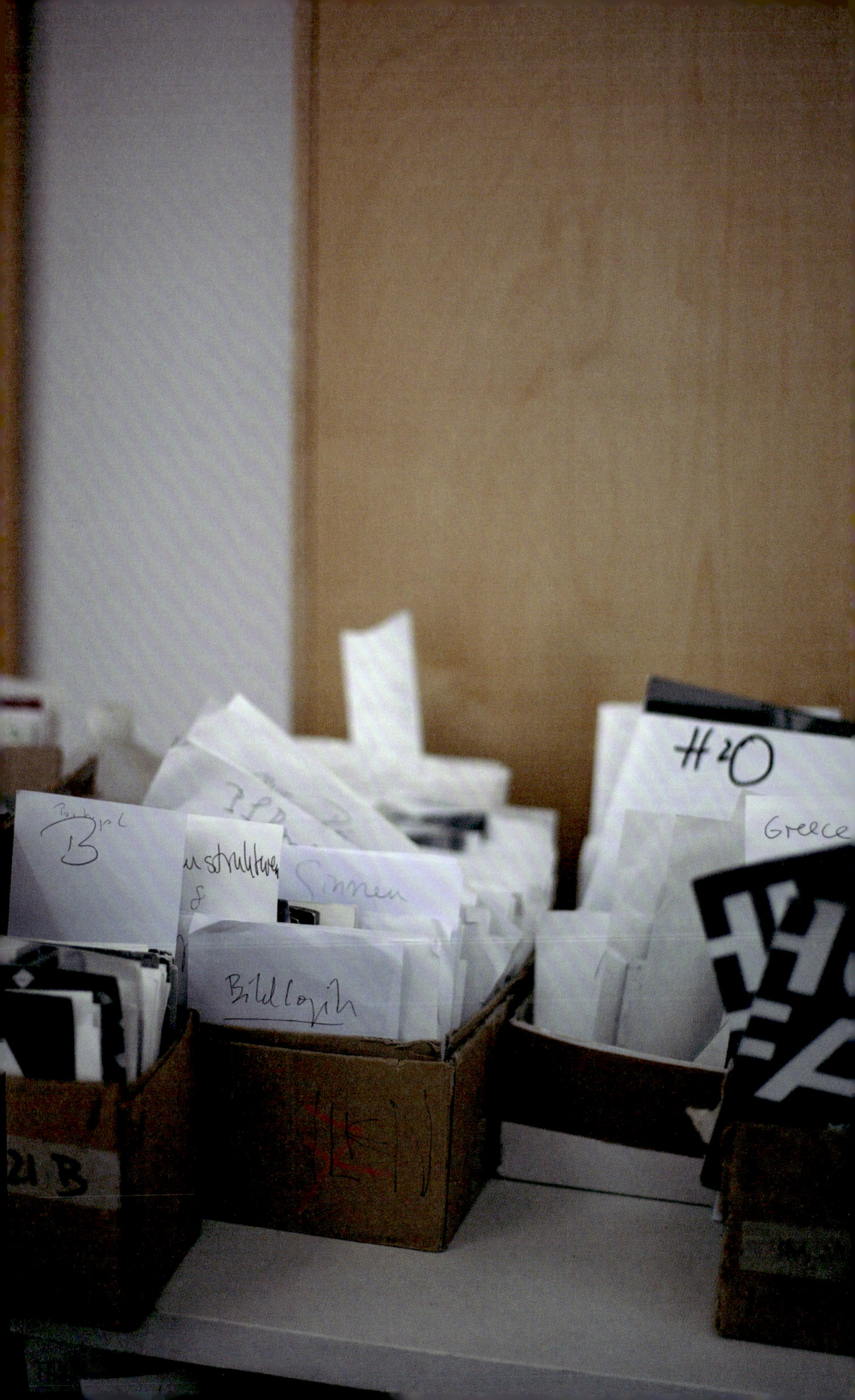
Greece
Sinnen
Bildlogik

Jochen Lempert, Hamburg 2021

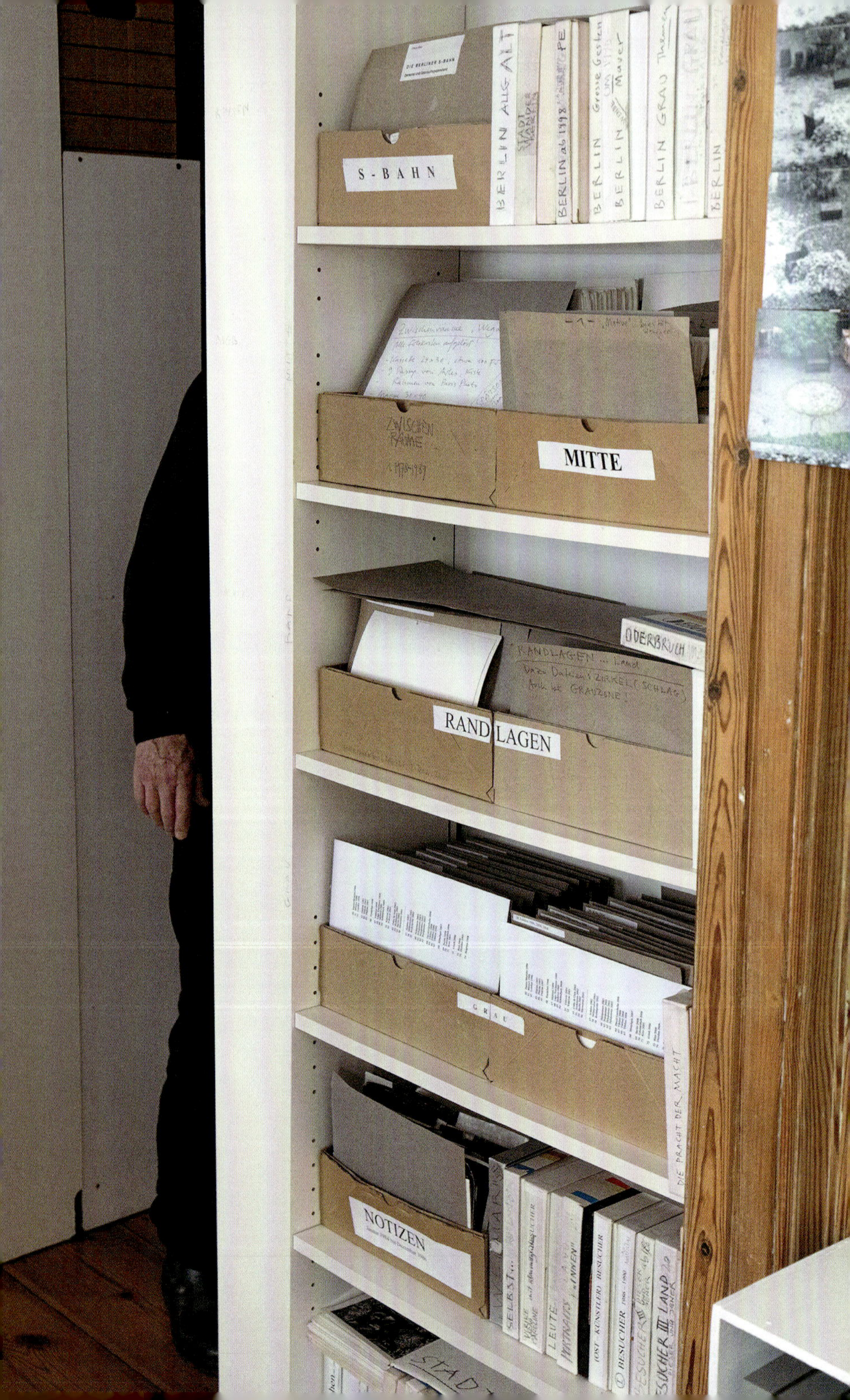
DIE BERLINER S-BAHN
S-BAHN
BERLIN AUS ALT
BERLIN GRAU
MITTE
ZWISCHENRÄUME
ODERBRUCH
RANDLAGEN
RAND LAGEN
GRAU
DIE PRACHT DER MACHT
NOTIZEN

Ulrich Wüst, Berlin 2021

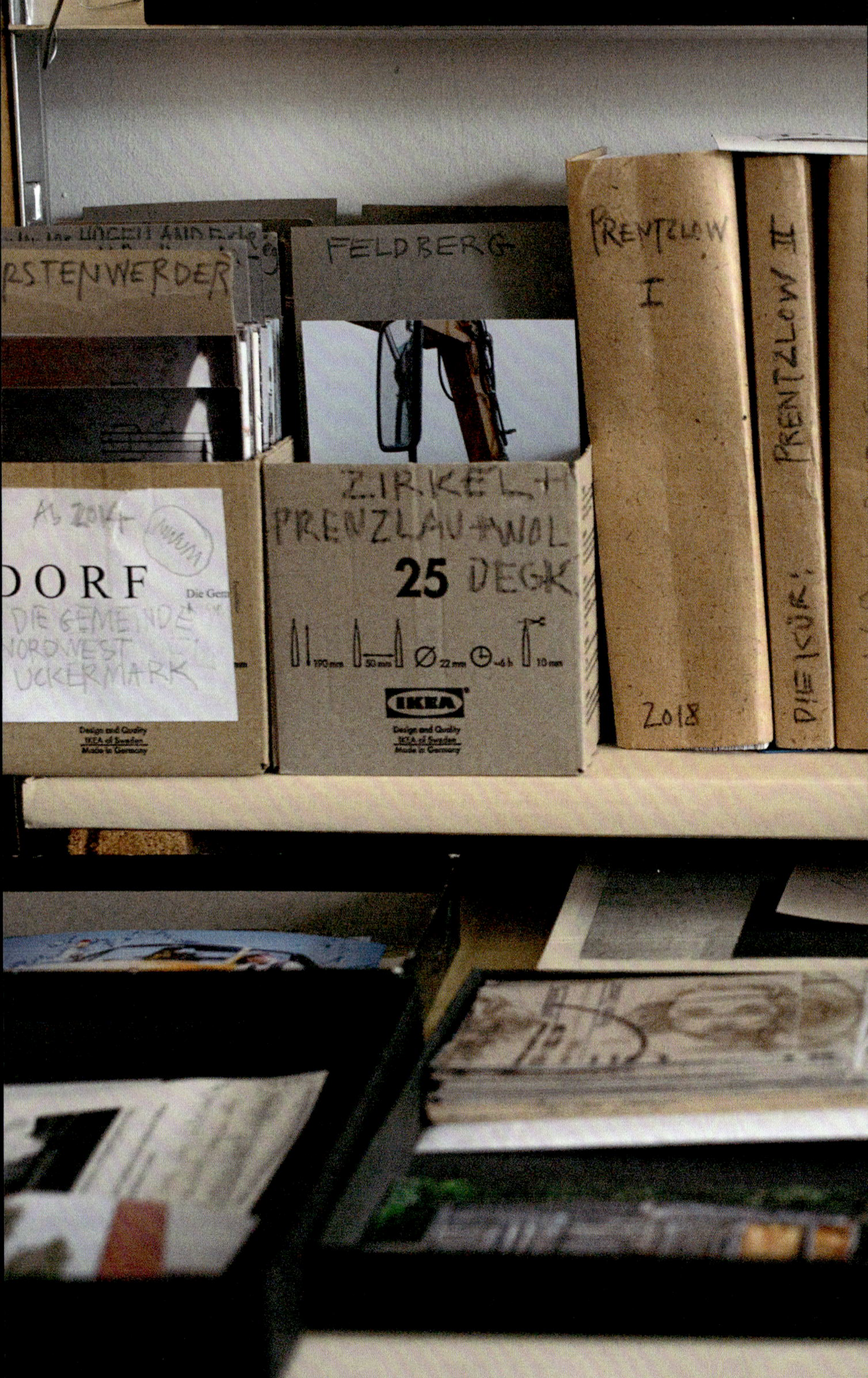
FELDBERG
PRENTZLOW
I
2018
PRENTZLOW II
DIE KÜR!
PRENZLAU
25
DORF
DIE GEMEINDE
NORDWEST
UCKERMARK
IKEA
Design and Quality
IKEA of Sweden
Made in Germany

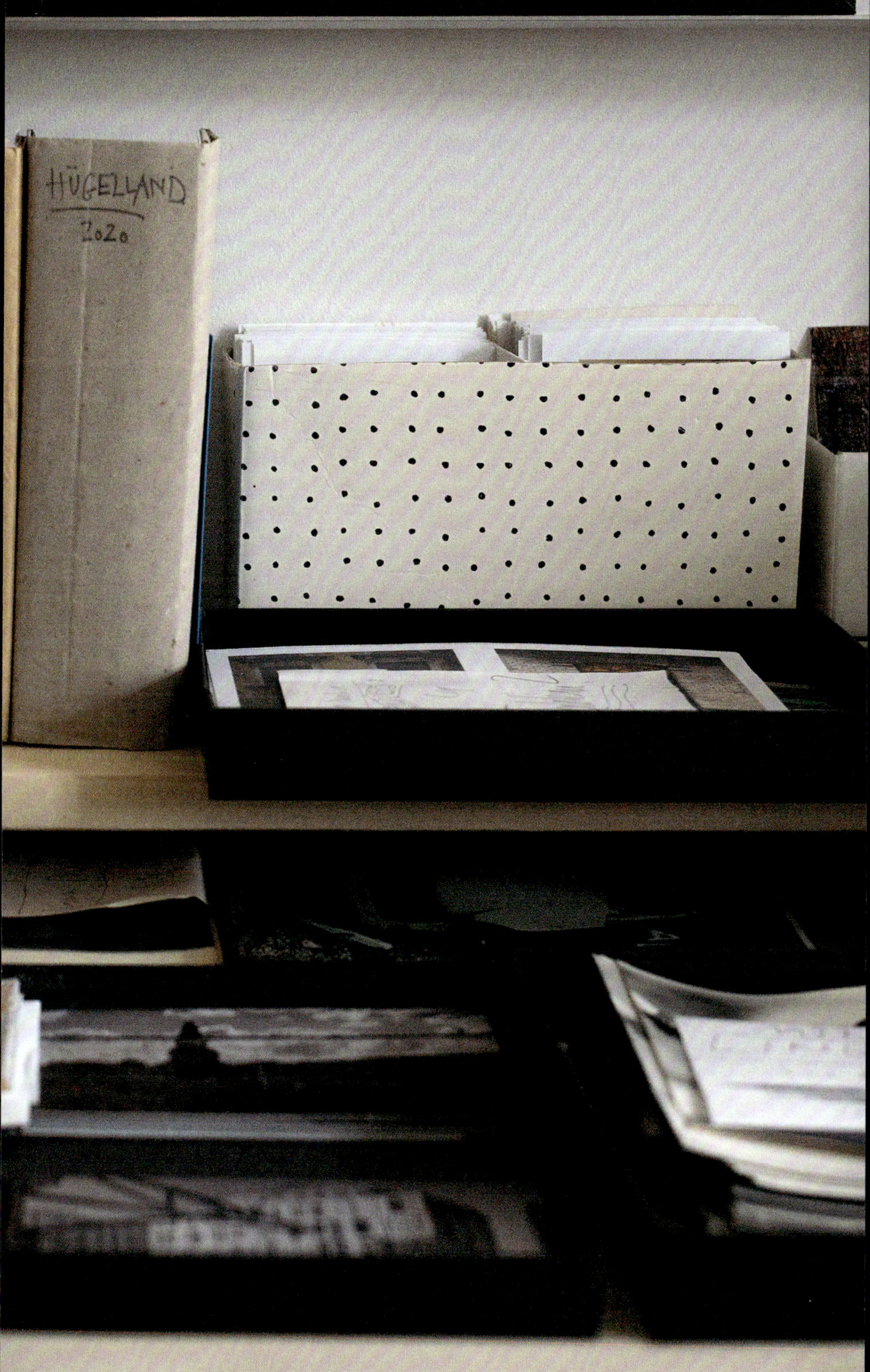
HÜGELLAND
2020

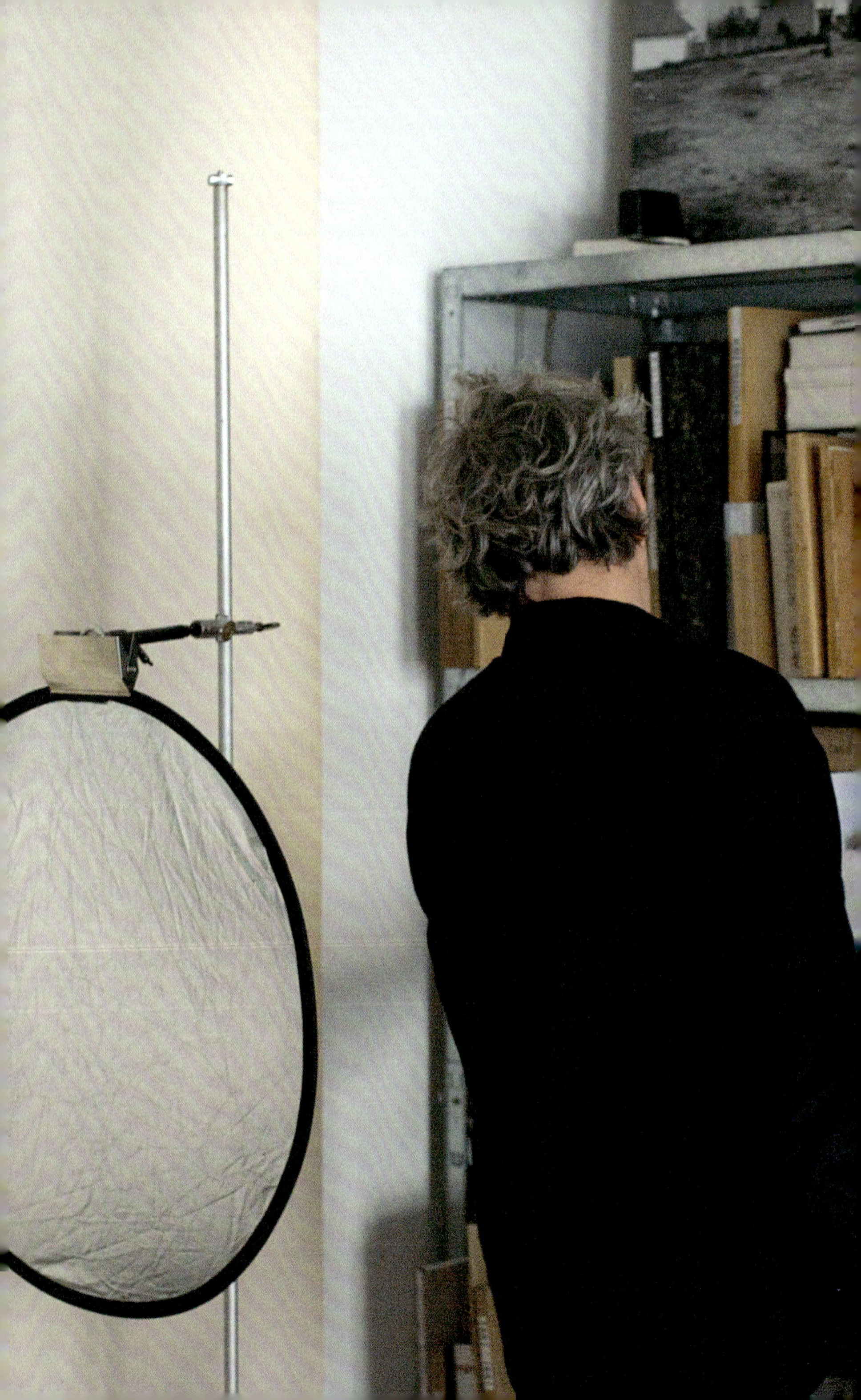

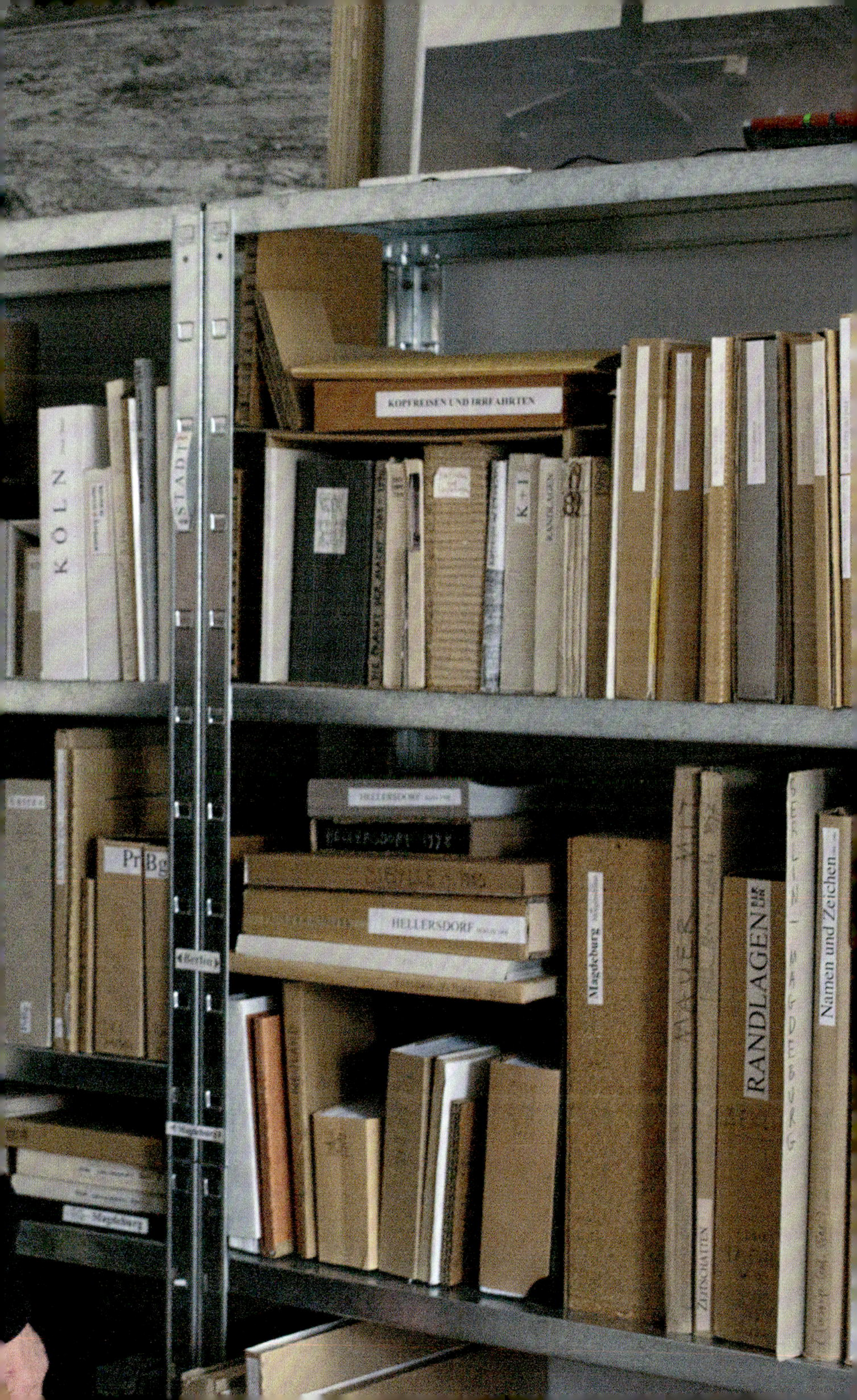

KOPFREISEN UND IRRFAHRTEN
KÖLN
HELLERSDORF
HELLERSDORF
Magdeburg
RANDLAGEN
Namen und Zeichen

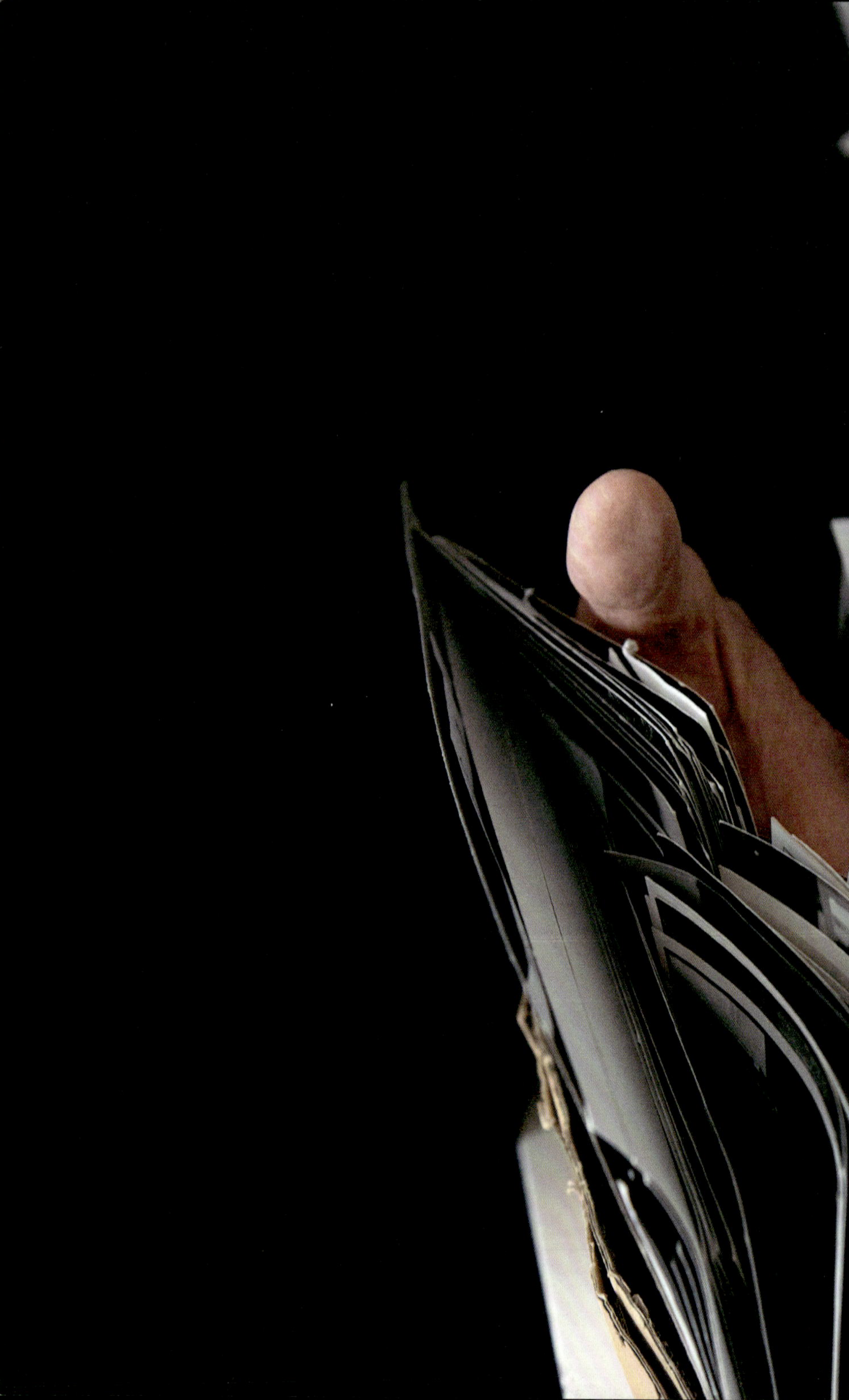

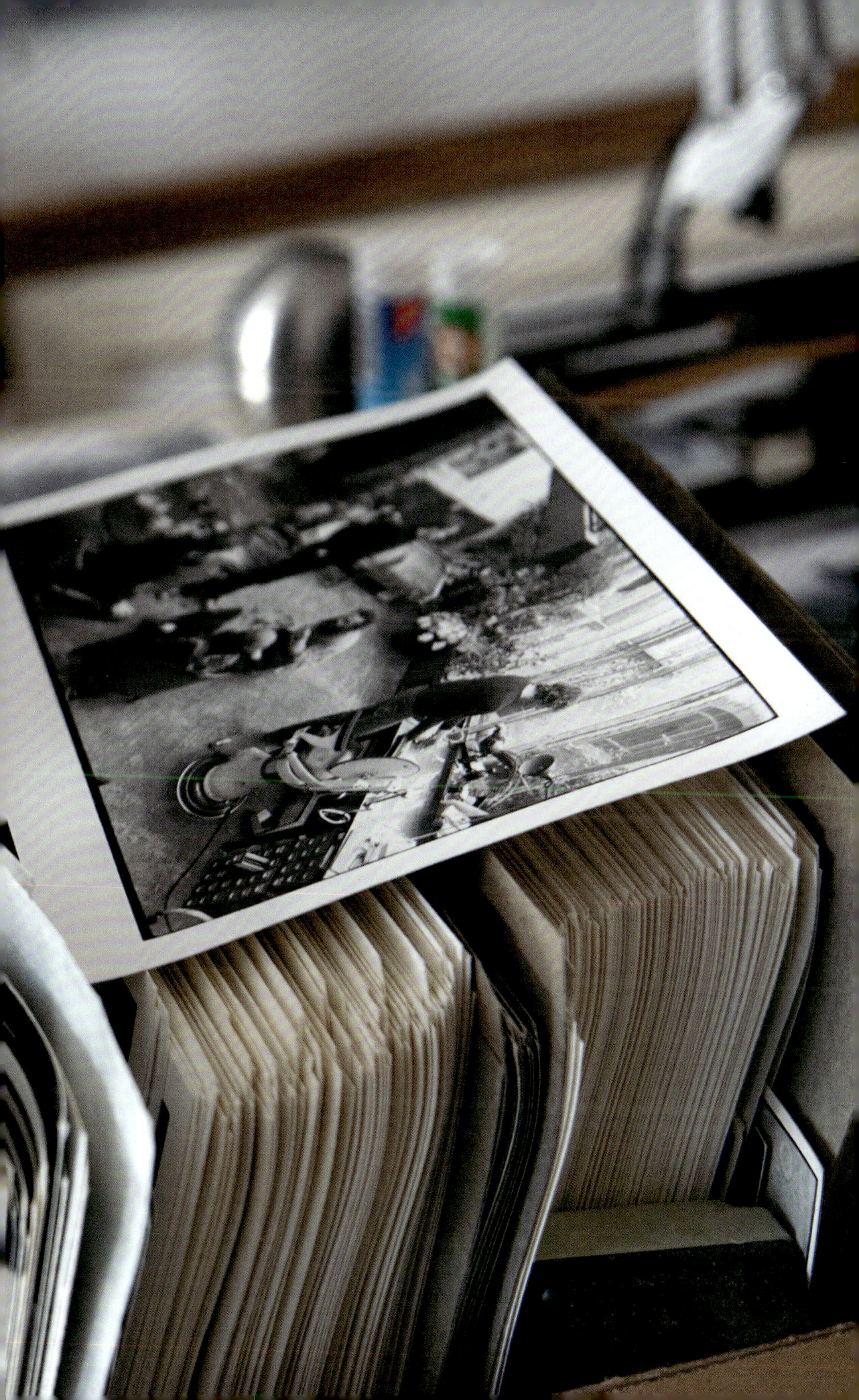

‘At some point, I’d like to be able to say
I did justice to the pictures.’
UTE MAHLER

‘It would simply be one worry less if my
things had a final destination.’
ULRICH WÜST

‘I would hope that the physical
works are managed in a
lively way.’
BEATE GÜTSCHOW

‘The archive is very important
because it’s the past in
the present.’
AKINBODE AKINBIYI

‘A good system and a good archive, really on point
and thought through, is almost a luxury asset.’
ANDREAS LANGFELD

'We no longer have the artist to tell us what can be scrapped and what can be shown.'
FRIEDA AND LILY VON WILD,
ESTATE SIBYLLE BERGEMANN

'An equitable archive will never exist anyway.
What does that even mean?'
PETER PILLER

'Archives are treasures. And the most interesting are archives whose deepest recesses have yet to be explored.'
ULRIKE KUSCHEL

'If photography can only enter a collection on the condition that it can no longer be shown as the artist intended, then it practically ceases to exist.'
WOLFGANG TILLMANS

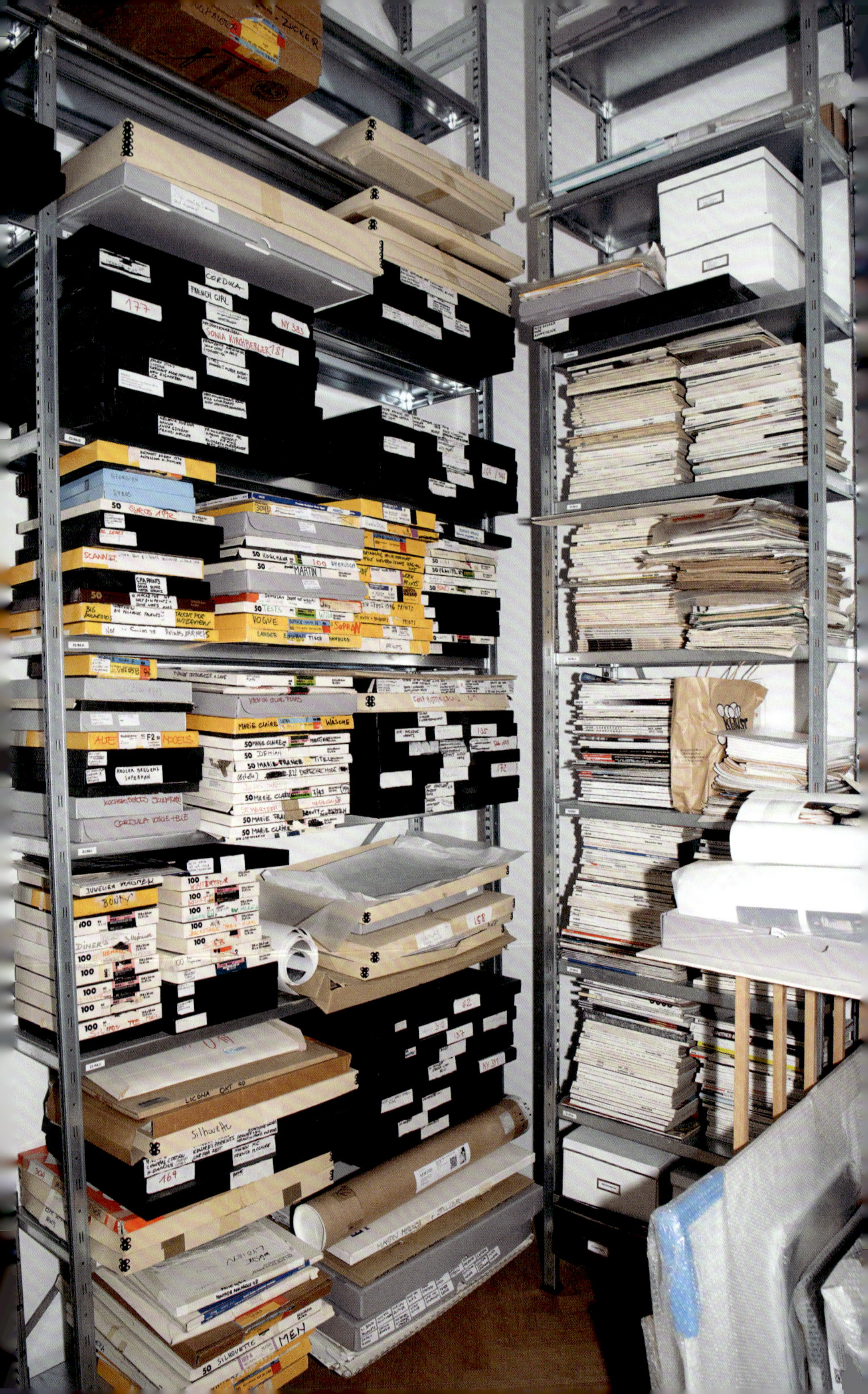
ZUCKER
CORDULA
FRENCH GIRL
177
NY 383
SONIA KIRCHBERGER 781
SCANNER
VOGUE
MARTIN
MARIE CLAIRE
WÄSCHE
MODELS
DEMIAN
JUWELIER WAGNER
BOUNTY
DINER
158
62
LICONA
Silhouette
169
SILHOUETTE
MEN

Elfie Semotan, Vienna 2021

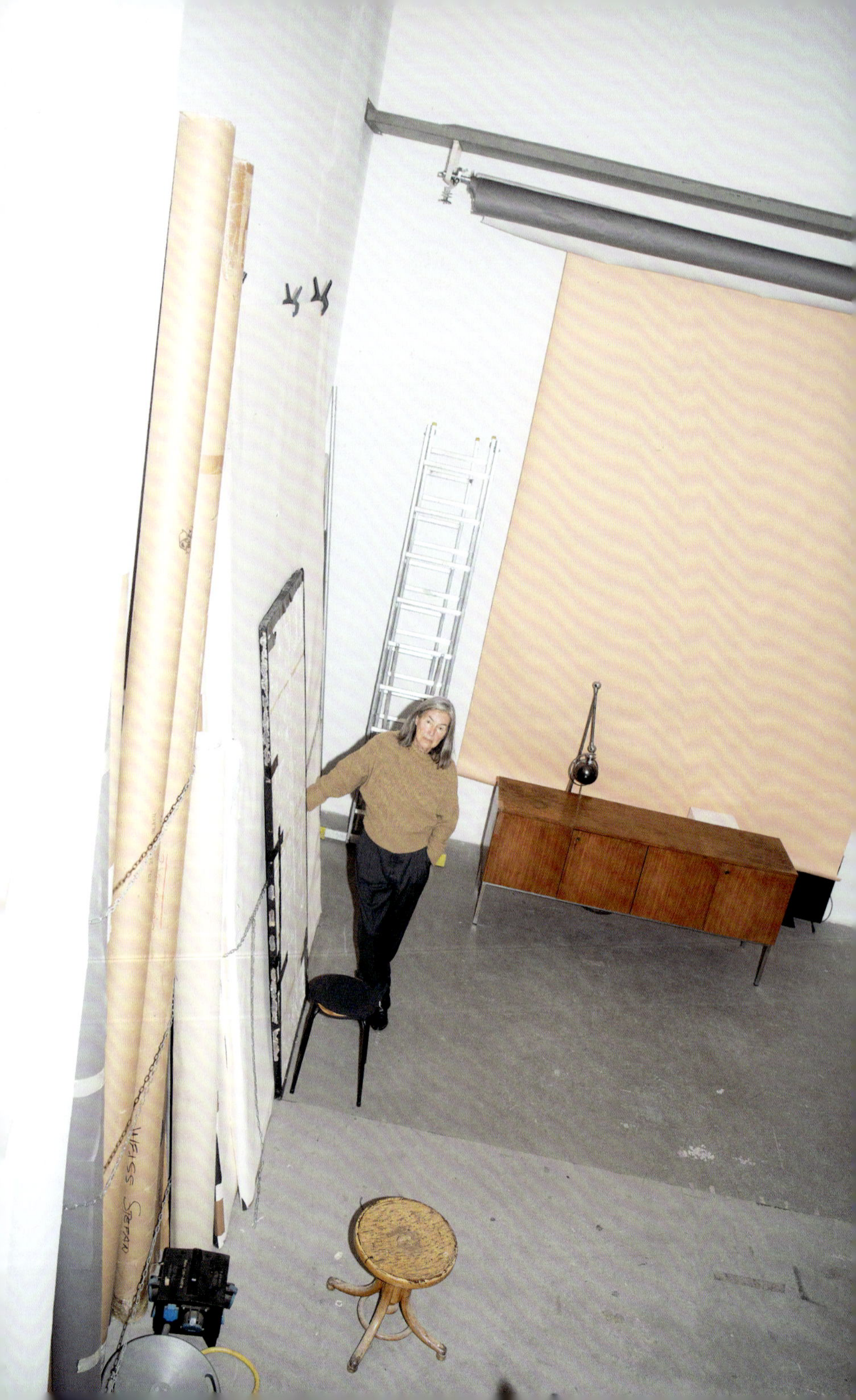
WEISS STEFAN

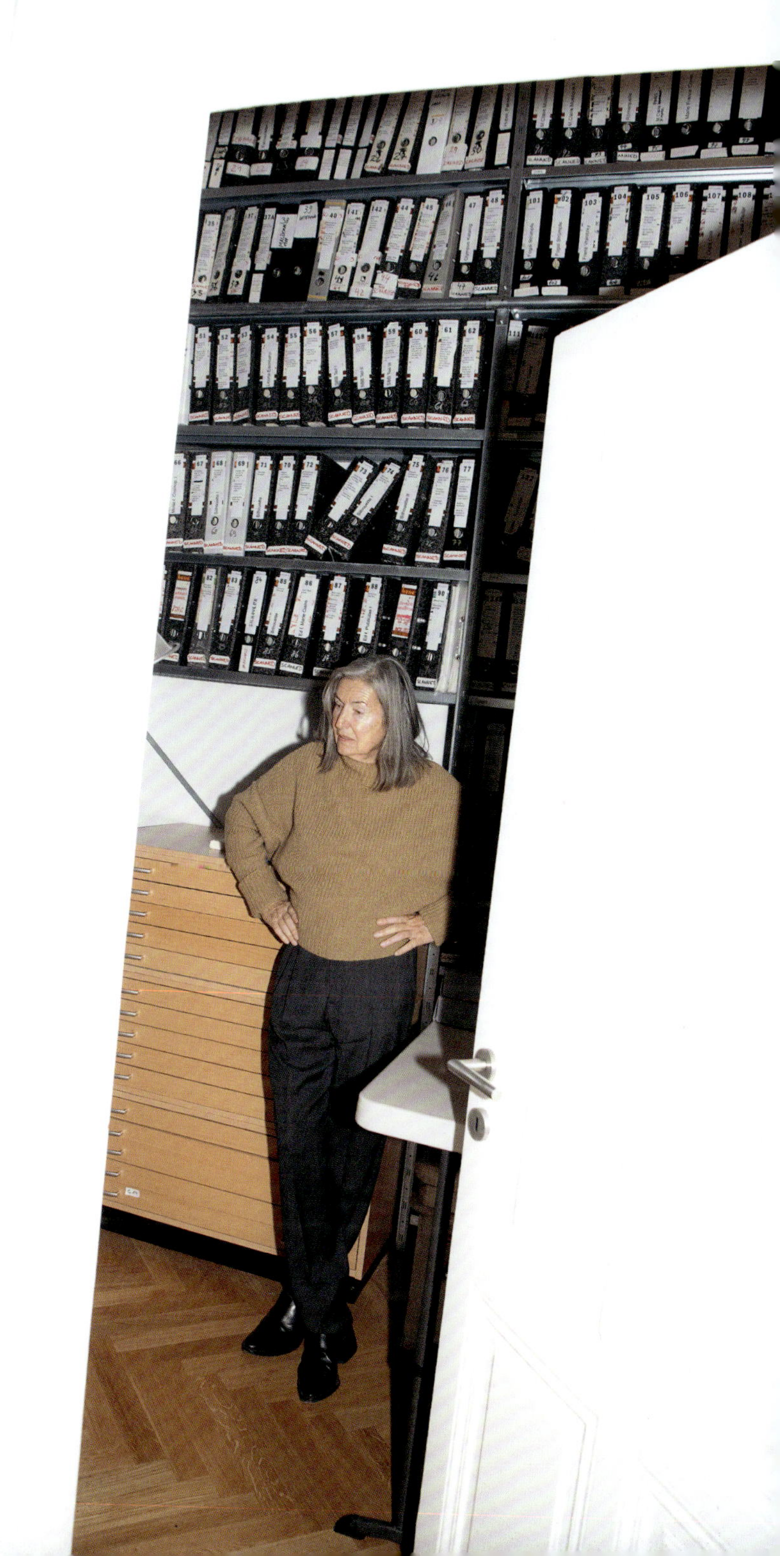

Lighting the Archive

Founded in 2020 by Heinz Peter Knes, Kristin Loschert, Maren Lübbke-Tidow, Heidi Specker, and Rebecca Wilton, the Lighting the Archive project conducts interviews that explore the ways the photographic is manifested and archived. All conversations and photographs can be found at www.lightingthearchive.org.

Mike Sperlinger

is a writer, curator, and Professor of Theory and Writing at the Oslo Academy of Fine Art, Norway. He has written extensively about the intersections between art, film and writing. He co-founded LUX, a London-based organisation for artists working with the moving image, and now runs PRISMS, a Norwegian non-profit for alternative film culture. He also looks after the artistic estate of Ian White and is the editor of the collection of White's writing, *Here is Information. Mobilise* (2016).

Available titles of the book series

Disss-co (A Fragment)
Douglas Crimp with Henrik Olesen
English edition

Tumbling Ruins
Henrike Naumann with Angela Schönberger and Andreas Brandolini
German and English edition

Tulips
Hannah Quinlan & Rosie Hastings with Christina B. Hanhardt
German and English edition

By The Highway
Ser Serpas with Rafik Greiss and Dora Budor
German and English edition

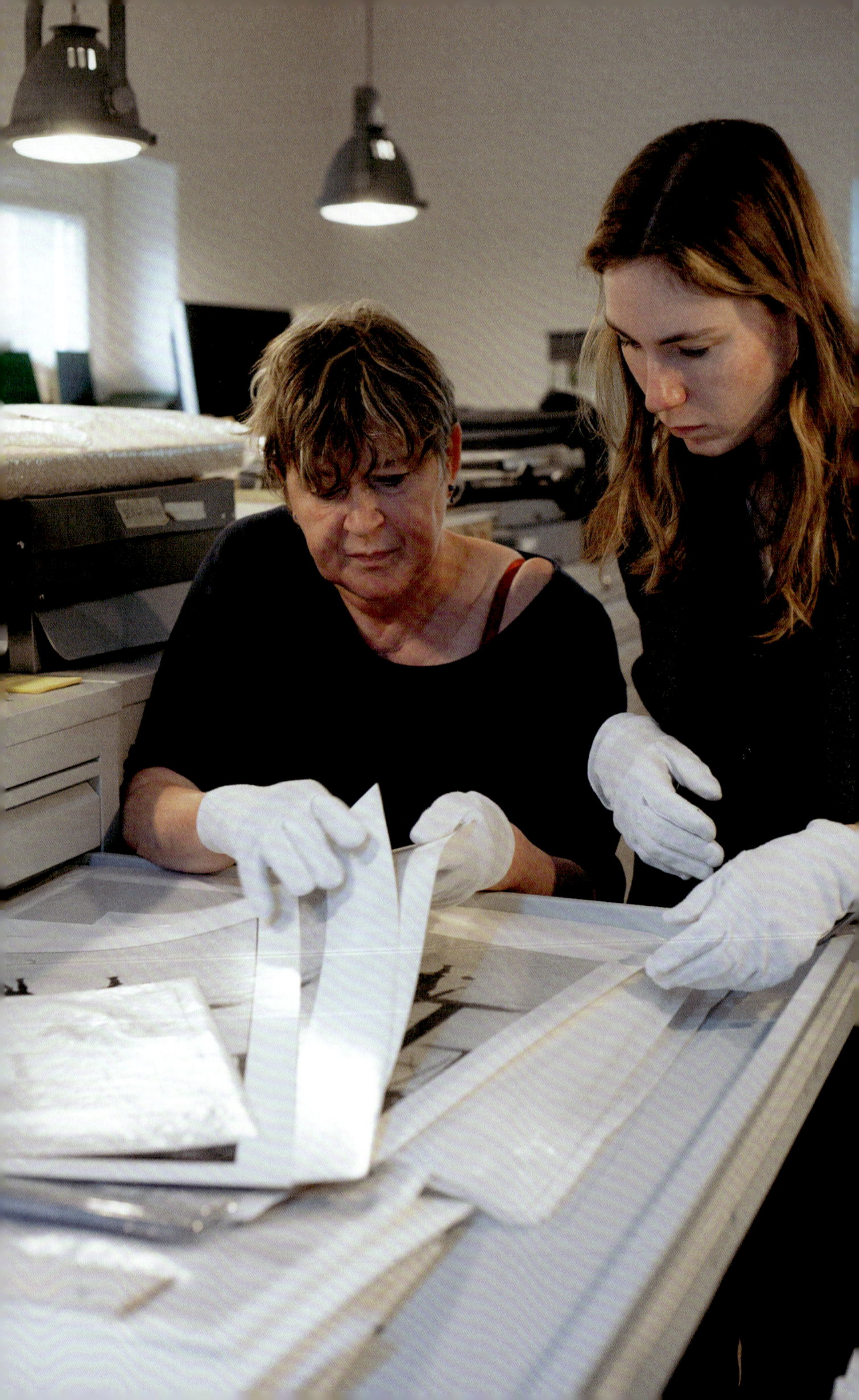

Estate Sibylle Bergemann, Margaretenhof 2022

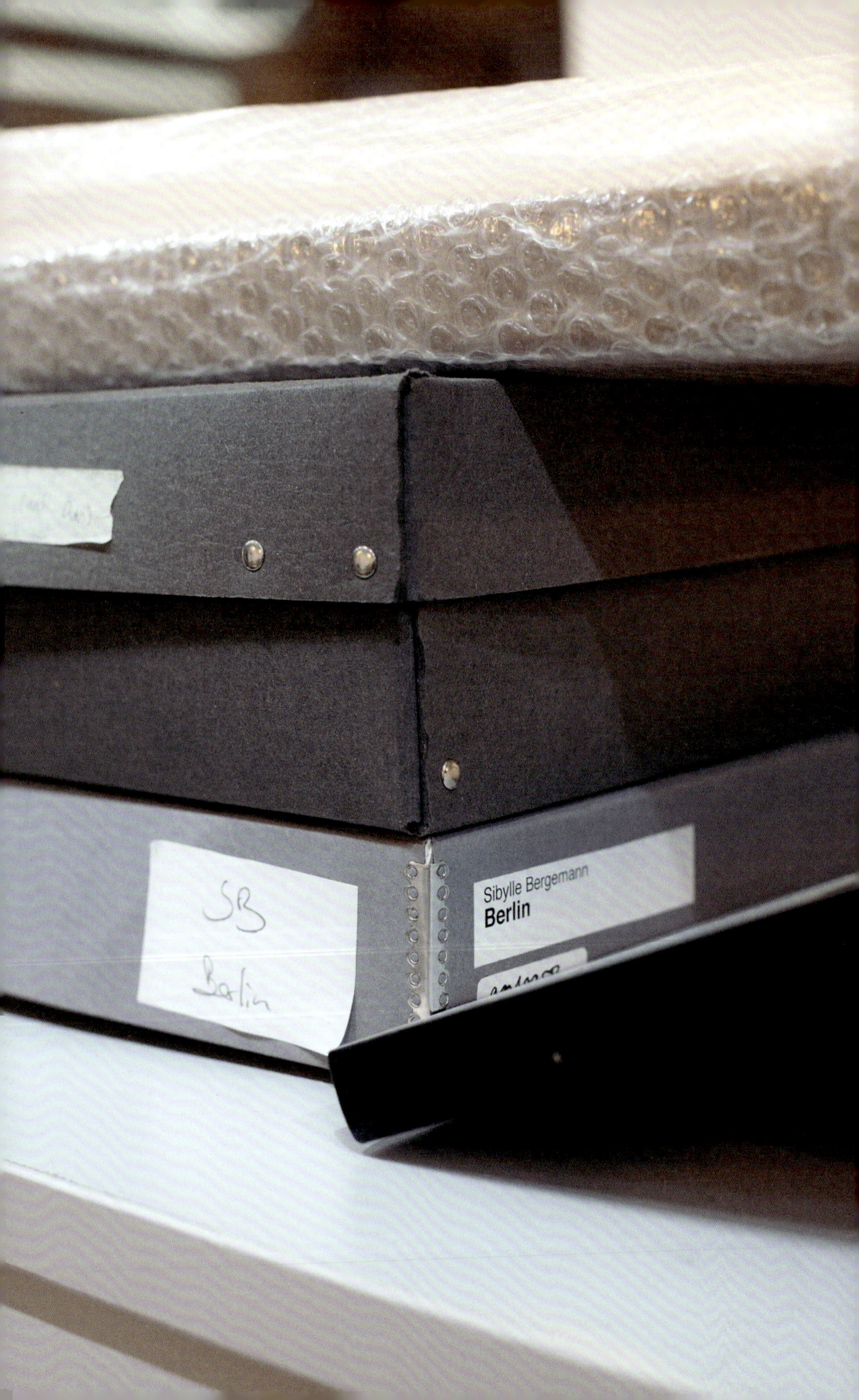
SB
Berlin
Sibylle Bergemann
Berlin

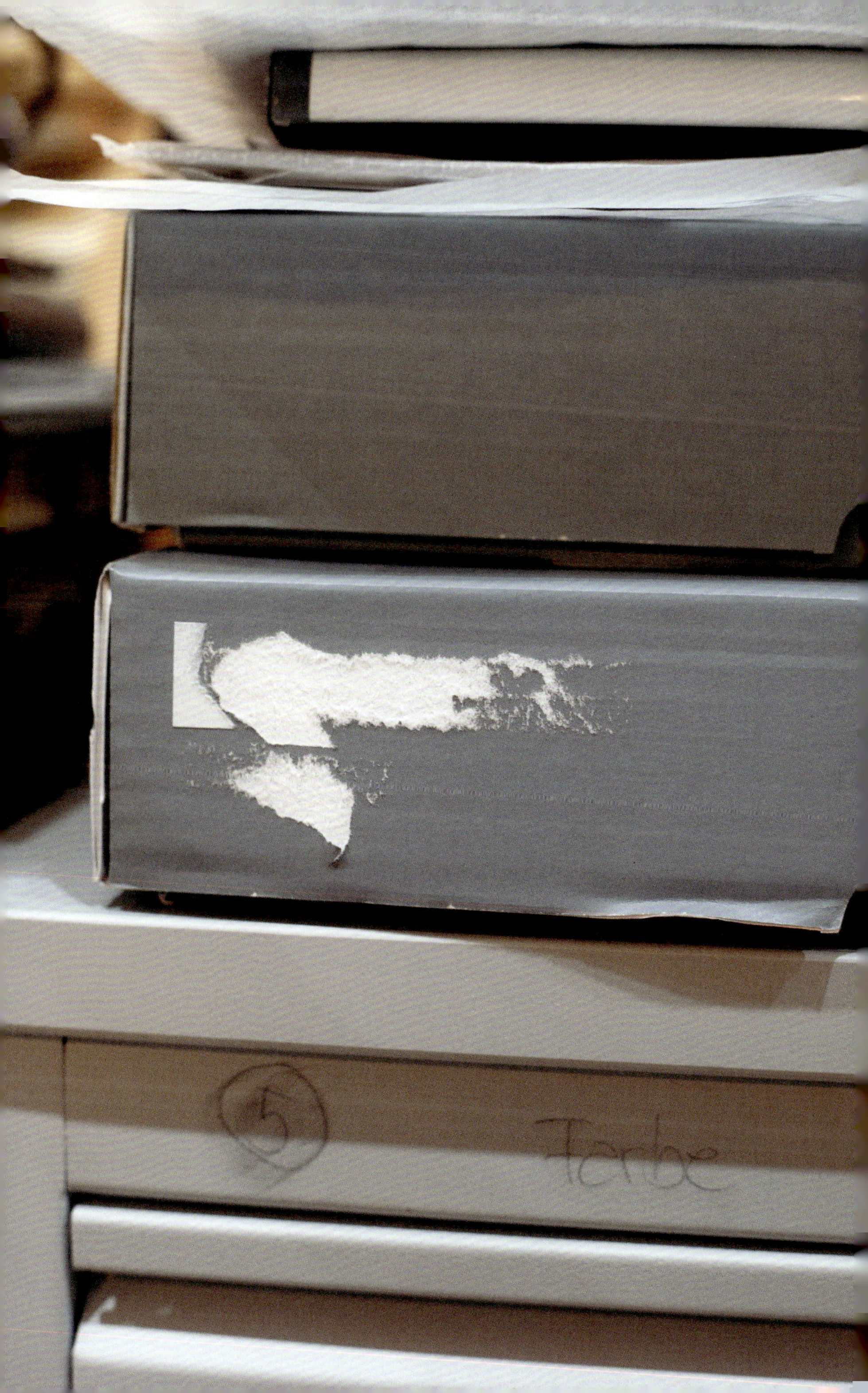
5
Farbe

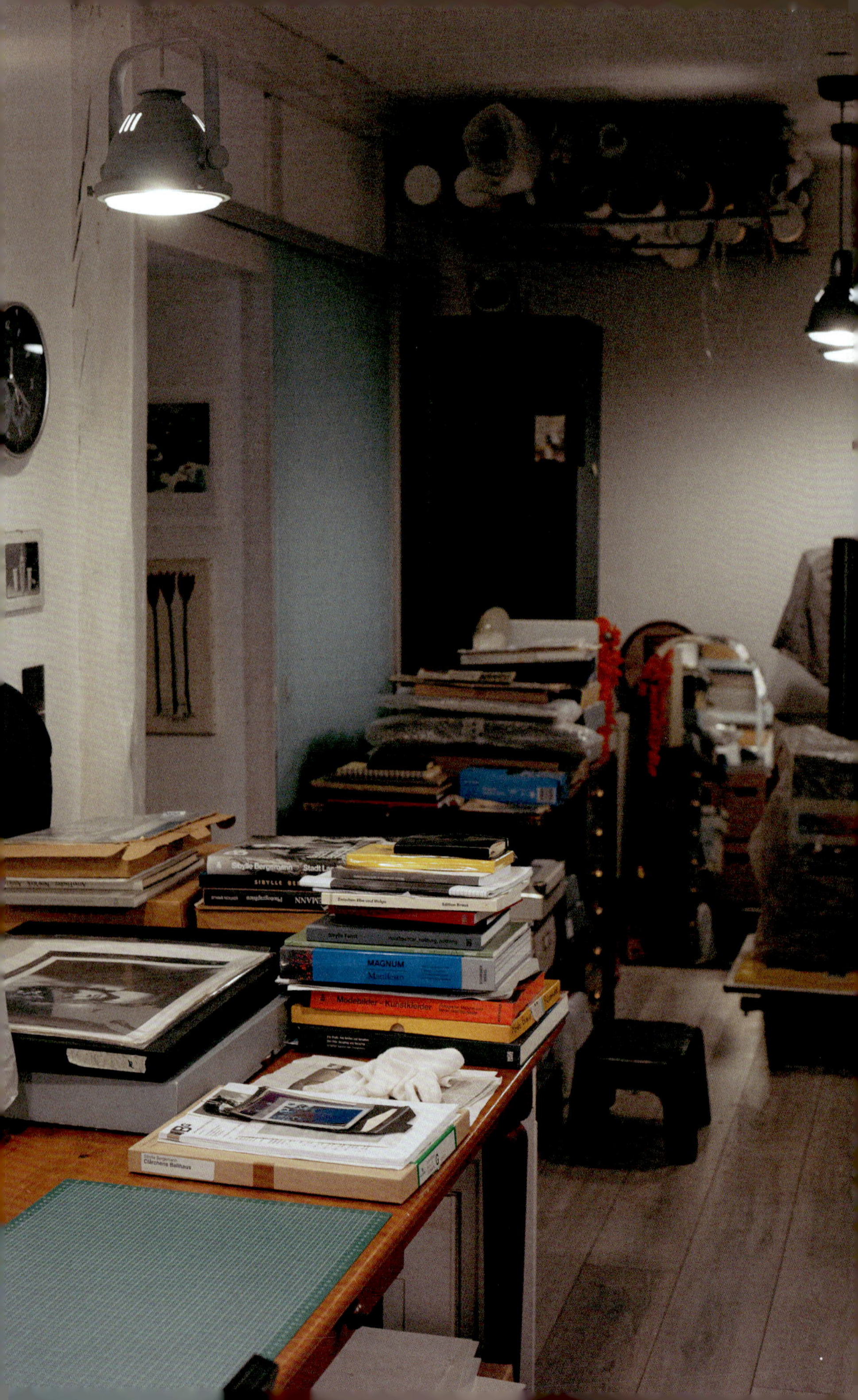
Sibylle Bergemann
Zwischen Elbe und Wolga
Edition Braus
MAGNUM
Modebilder – Kunstkleider
Sibylle Bergemann
Clärchens Ballhaus

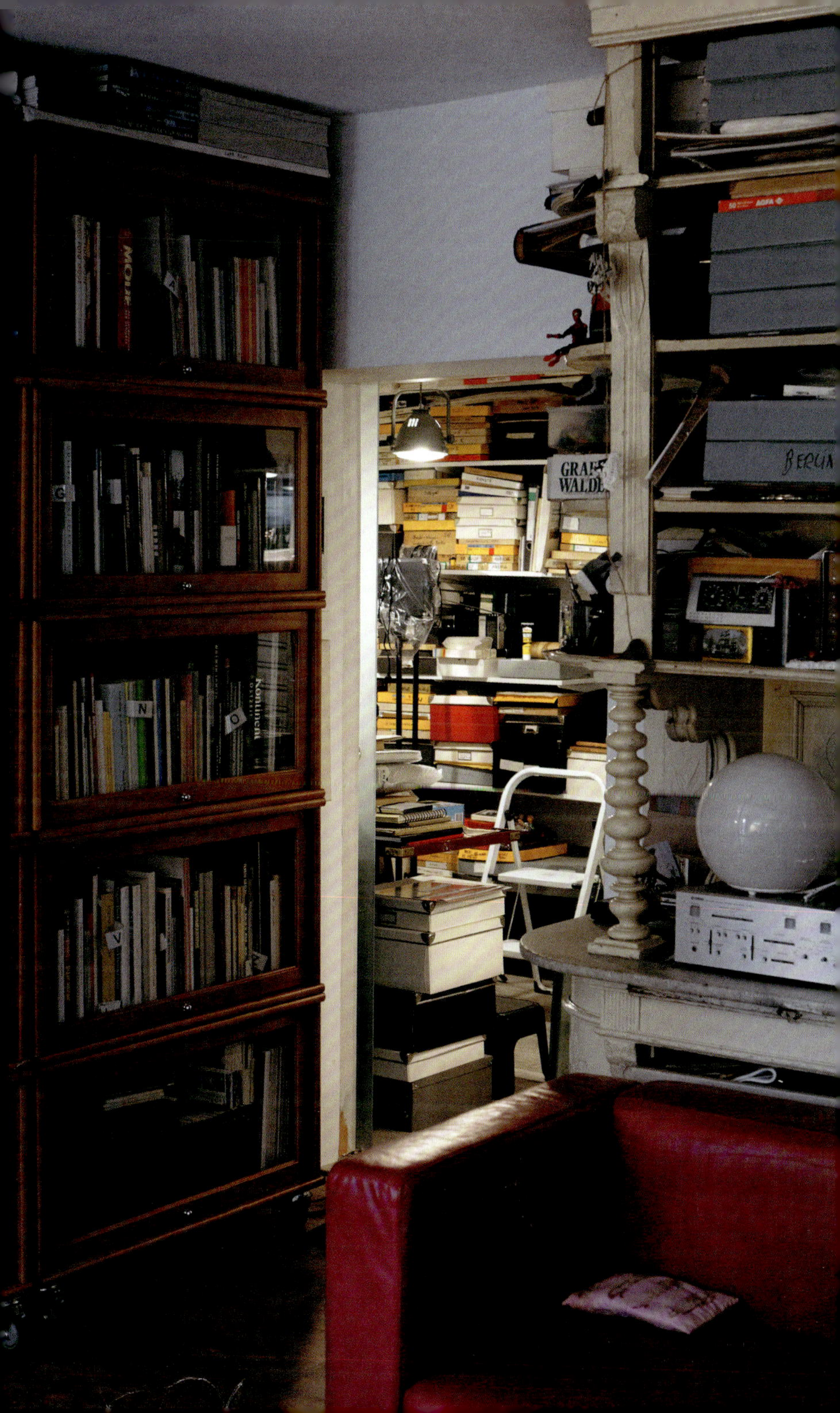

KONTEXT is a series by DISTANZ.

Acknowledgments

Matthias Kliefoth would like to thank Lighting the Archive and Mike Sperlinger as well as Tanya Leighton Gallery.

Lighting the Archive would like to thank all artists and photographers who place their trust in the project, open their studios and present their working methods.

Colophon

Editors
Matthias Kliefoth, Rebecca Wilton

Design
Manuel Tayarani

Essay
Mike Sperlinger

Copy Editing
Nicholas Grindell, Matthias Kliefoth

Photo Credits
All images by Rebecca Wilton, except: Kristin Loschert, pp. 50–53; Heinz Peter Knes, pp. 90–97; Maria Ziegelböck, pp. 100–103

Image Editing
Reproline mediateam

Production Management
Charlotte Riggert

Printing and Binding
Druckhaus Sportflieger, Berlin

ISBN 978-3-95476-486-0
Printed in Germany

Published by
DISTANZ Verlag
www.distanz.de

This book is also published in a German edition.